TAKING STOCK

A Hospice Doctor's Advice on
Financial Independence,
Building Wealth, and Living
a Regret-Free Life

JORDAN GRUMET, MD

Published by:
Ulysses Press
PO Box 3440
Berkeley, CA 94703
www.ulyssespress.com

ISBN: 978-1-64604-354-5
Library of Congress Control Number: 2022932299

Printed in the United States by Versa Press
10 9 8 7 6 5 4 3 2

Acquisitions editor: Claire Sielaff
Managing editor: Claire Chun
Editor: Cathy Cambron
Proofreader: Renee Rutledge
Front cover design: Chris Cote
Cover artwork: from shutterstock.com—gold background © janniwet; coin © Hierarch
Interior design and layout: Winnie Liu
Interior artwork: from shutterstock.com—chapter graphics © Nova II; part coins

© sensvector; graphs © Mind Pixell; Maslow's pyramid, page 20 © mayrum; arrow graphic, page 22 © PUWADON SANG

For Harriet, Alan, and Gerald.
Not everyone is lucky enough to get three great parents.

CONTENTS

IMPORTANT NOTE TO THE READER

FOREWORD

Jordan Grumet discovered the secret key to the financial independence retire early (FIRE) movement. This secret key has little to do with money. It has nothing to do with retirement. It has nothing to do with freedom from work. And while it is definitely about time, it's not about being early or late.

I met Jordan in the summer of 2019, when he invited me to be on his *Earn & Invest* podcast. Reluctantly, I agreed. While I've liked FIRE podcasters and bloggers, I have had little to offer on their passionate interests—building wealth through investing—but a lot to say about my environmental and social values, which often seemed off topic. But Jordan was different. He set up the conversation talking about justice and privilege.

When he offered me a chance to write this introduction, I gladly said yes.

Jordan's book introduces you to a man who had the courage to exit the dominant paradigm of "making a living" to spend his time looking at living and dying through the eyes of his hospice patients.

He applied—and teaches—the techniques of the FIRE movement, but this is not a financial independence retire early book.

FINANCIAL

While Jordan talks about his financial decisions, his message is that money is a poor way to meet our needs for love, purpose, personal growth, introspection, and service. Meeting those nonmaterial needs, it turns out, determines how deep and satisfying our lives become. While Jordan "had it made" financially as a medical doctor, he was impoverished until he let go of his practice and focused on the most meaningful part of his work:

serving hospice patients in their last weeks and days. He managed his money wisely and does teach about his methods, but his teaching is about putting money in service to his values and true happiness.

INDEPENDENCE

The dream of independence, of saying "take this job and shove it" to a dead-end job, is very attractive. It's what gets most people into the FIRE movement. Leaving a job that's killing you, though, doesn't make you free. It just gives you free time, which you then have to figure out how to fill. The empty canvas of time requires you to ask, What is truly worthy of my time and attention? As a hospice doctor who serves people for whom time has just about run out, Jordan considers this question every day. How shall I live? Where shall I lay up my treasure? When I am the one in that bed, struggling to breathe, what will make me feel that my life was well spent? Such questions have nothing to do with bucket lists, yoga classes, or destinations. Instead, these questions have to do with introspection, humility, and caring for more than me and mine.

RETIRE

Retirement is an artifact of industrialization. We have become cogs in a machine that leaves people more dead than alive at the end of the day. Joe Dominguez, originator of the program in our book, *Your Money or Your Life*, used to say, "People aren't making a living. If they were, they'd be more alive at the end of the day. No, they are making a dying." Our book, and the FIRE teachers, show a discipline that, followed loyally, leads to a way out of this grind.

Buddhist economics considers that there are three purposes of work:

1. To provide for your material needs

2. To develop character

3. To make a contribution to the community

We are social animals, not just self-improving individuals. We want to contribute. Our work may change from earning money to activism, volunteering, the arts, inventing, a new career, or helping others, but we still work, and the work makes us whole. Retirement conjures a life of relaxation, playing golf perhaps, being a snowbird in a motor home, or babysitting grandchildren. All of these activities can be fun—but in moderation and not as the whole meal. We want to apply ourselves to things that matter not just to us but to others as well.

Amartya Sen, Nobel Prize–winning economist, said: "Poverty is not just a lack of money; it is not having the capability to realize one's full potential as a human being."

Freedom isn't entitlement to do as you please. It's agency to do as you value.

Jordan retired from a way of life that had no real joy in it and reinvested his life energy in what lit up his heart and soul.

For me this reinvestment came several years into my own financial independence, when I learned about the ecological principle of "overshoot and collapse": any species with an ample food source and no predators will grow in numbers and eat through the food until there isn't enough to support the population of the species. Then the population collapses. I saw clearly, nearly fifty years ago, that our human community was headed off such a cliff, and it's been my privilege to use my freedom to create, write, organize, volunteer, speak, and influence others as much as I could to change our course. Every minute has challenged, stimulated, and grown me toward my full humanity. No minute was aimed at earning money, as I'd learned to live within the income I had from cautious investments.

EARLY

And now for "early." Life is not a race to a finish line. It's not a competition. There is no gold medal. Winning is directing your life energy toward what you most value and what brings you the deepest joy. I think the promise of *earliness* is part of the American pipe dream, of frontiers, winning, outcompeting, success. We are a country of immigrants who all got away from somewhere and something: kings, famines, pogroms, wars. We are also a country that has not reckoned with the problem that some people's freedom has been other people's terrible loss of freedom. The great law of freedom is that we are free to act, but we are not free of the consequences—good and bad—of our actions. I see Jordan as having matured from a life not to his liking and into acceptance that "no man is an island, separated from the whole."

For some in the FIRE community, Jordan's decision to sacrifice income for meaning, and retirement for service to the dying, makes little sense: He should make as much as possible as soon as possible and leave the meaning part to after retirement. Then he could have all the meaning he wants. His example, though, and the evolution of many people in his networks have opened up conversations about how FIRE relates to justice, capitalism's discontents, privilege, compassion, generosity, and the common good.

The definition of "FIRE" is evolving. There's now fat FIRE (passive income equal to your highest earning year), lean FIRE (passive income equal to your more frugal spending), barista FIRE (passive income plus a part-time job for the benefits), and coast FIRE (earning enough, early enough, to invest it and let it grow into enough to retire later while you work less frantically).

Perhaps, after reading this book, "FIRE" will translate into "financial integrity" and "retire eventually"—or maybe "respond with empathy," "realize enlightenment," "rescue the earth," "restore equity," or "reflect on eternity."

In Jordan's chosen work, that last action is a daily affair.

Vicki Robin, coauthor of *Your Money or Your Life*
October 2021

* * *

The stories I share in *Taking Stock* are all based on my experiences with patients at the end of life. I have changed identifying details and used composite stories in order to protect patient confidentiality.

—Jordan Grumet

PART ONE

WHAT FINANCIAL INDEPENDENCE EXPERTS GET WRONG ABOUT LIFE—AND DEATH

INTRODUCTION

When I was seven, my father died suddenly, unexpectedly. I remember a lot about the day it happened: the fluorescent lights in the principal's office while I waited to be picked up, the look on my mother's friend Noel's face when she arrived at school, the words my mother whispered later that day that would change my life forever.

"He's gone."

I also remember that his death just didn't make any sense. I was at an age when I worshiped my father. I tried to walk the way he did. I copied his facial expressions and words. How could this young man, this doctor, this *superhero* just collapse one day and cease to exist, leaving behind not only a wife, but also my two older brothers and me?

How could he leave? It was a question I asked myself over and over again in the weeks that followed. Like most young children, I interpreted the world through a fairly self-centered lens, and so I wondered whether the answer to that question was *me*—maybe I wasn't good enough, smart enough, or lovable enough.

The answer to all my questions came a few months later in the form of a dream. I was standing in the hospital wearing my father's lab coat and stethoscope. Nurses and patients flew past me in a flurry as I calmly helped those in need. I was good. I was whole. I was able to fill the place my father left vacant.

We tell ourselves the stories about our lives that make it bearable—or, better yet, magical, mystical. And, finally, I had a story that made sense. I would become a doctor like my father. I convinced myself that walking in his footsteps would cosmically fix the mistake of his death, a mistake that I was somehow responsible for.

This story carried me far. It carried me through a learning disorder that threatened my ability to read. It carried me through a childhood devoid of close friendships and through failures in athletics and, eventually, relationships. It pushed me to study for hours while others were enjoying themselves or watching television. It was not a question of *if* I would become a doctor, but when.

By the time I reached college, I had grown into the student I had always wanted to be. I could sit with a textbook for hours and absorb the most difficult and challenging material. I attacked my bachelor's degree with the certitude that it would swiftly lead to a place in medical school and, eventually, residency. I was living my dreams or, at least, what I thought my dreams should be.

It would soon, however, become progressively difficult to ignore the signs that maybe I wasn't living the dream I thought I was. One of those signs came on my first day on the job at a residency program in internal medicine at Washington University in 1999. At the end of my tour around the hospital, a residency director introduced me to the third-year resident who was ready to hand off his patients to me.

"This is John," the director said. "You'll be taking his place. He can't be hurt anymore."

I was confused. *Can't be hurt anymore? What the heck does that mean? Who is hurting him?* It would take me a year to understand what those words meant: what a continual assault on the psyche it is to work in an intensive care unit. Building walls was my way of girding myself against the sleeplessness, the militant hierarchy of the medical profession, and the pain I felt when accepting that harsh but fundamental truth of medicine: some patients cannot be saved. I learned how to sublimate my emotions, fears, and sadness to such an extent that they became almost nonexistent.

Almost.

I probably would have continued doctoring on autopilot if not for the day my son was born: October 25, 2004. When I held him in my arms in the delivery room, I felt the walls I had so expertly built start to tumble down. I could no longer protect myself from all that was painful because in the process I would also be blocking out all the love and joy I felt for my son, for my wife, for humanity. I had to accept that death—the death of my father, my patients, and even someday my own—was just as natural as the newborn wiggling in my arms.

I went back to work with a new sense of vigor. I learned how to both laugh and cry with my patients. I stopped trying to avoid all that was painful about doctoring and chose to embrace it. Yet, in the process, I learned something that would truly change my understanding of the dream I'd had so many years earlier.

On a sunny spring day shortly after graduating medical school, I was helping my mother sort through a pile of long-forgotten boxes in the attic. Unexpectedly, I stumbled across a few of my father's old papers that my mom had kept from his training days. As I perused his notebooks, I could sense a love and joy for the material that was so meticulously laid down on the pages. Graphs were painstakingly copied and labeled with accuracy and care. It was clear he had an innate love for the science, which I never shared.

For me, it was the people and relationships that I fell in love with. My happiest moments were when I was able to act toward my patients as suggested by the original Latin from which the word "doctor" derives: *docere*, to teach. I was at my best when I was explaining the magnificence of the human body and its impermanence: how and why it falters.

But was being a physician the only way I could achieve these goals?

The question frightened me. After spending so many years pursuing this path and practicing medicine, it was jarring to come to the conclusion that I had chosen unwisely—so jarring, in fact, that I tried just about everything to avoid that conclusion.

I quit working for a medical group and started my own practice because I thought control was what I was lacking. This move quelled my fears briefly, but it didn't take me long to realize that I no longer enjoyed office medicine. My next solution was to leave the office and start a concierge medical practice in which I saw patients in their own homes.

While this model was quite streamlined and profitable, it was only a few years before the same demons overtook me. I was burned out and unhappy, experiencing too little sleep and too much work in a profession that was giving me very little joy. I had no idea what to do with my career and no idea which direction my life should take.

Completely by coincidence, around this time, a physician author contacted me to review his financial book for my medical blog. His book, which I read in one sitting, introduced me to the concept of financial independence and connected a number of disparate economic concepts that I had failed to tie together previously. I hadn't realized that there was a whole group of people, the financial independence retire early (FIRE) community, that helped individuals like me learn how to calculate how much money they need to live without ever making another cent.

After I did the math, I realized that I was free. Because of good financial habits my parents had modeled for me as a kid, I had saved enough money to support myself for the rest of my life without worrying about what I did for a living. Just like the FIRE devotees that I read about, I had embraced the mantra of frugality, saving, and investing wisely. I owned real estate as well as my own thriving business. I already had enough money and sources of income to retire early.

It was the other aspect of the FIRE equation, though, that unexpectedly brought tears to my eyes. What these financial experts were telling me was that from this very day it was possible to fill my time only with activities that were most consistent with my true desires.

But...what were those desires?

This should have been one of the happiest moments of my life, but my joy at the prospect of leaving medicine was quickly replaced with both sorrow and fear. Sorrow at feeling the last wisps of my connection with my father fade away and fear that maybe I didn't have the faintest idea what my true desires really were.

I did know that I didn't really share my father's innate love of the science of medicine. I knew that I didn't want to feel the pain and loss of his passing anymore. And I knew that I didn't want to die young like he had.

This was, at least, a start. Those thoughts had taken up so much mental space—had, in fact, driven many of my behaviors over the years—that they left little room to divine my own innate calling. But when it came to how I really wanted to spend my time, when I thought about what I wanted my legacy on this earth to be, I came up short.

I knew I needed to dive deeper. And I felt a sense of urgency when it came to figuring all this out because my kids were starting to get older. I wanted them to look up to me the same way I did my father. I wanted to make sure they had everything they needed for a secure future no matter what happened. It was never lost on me that my career in medicine and my midlife shift were in part funded by my father's life insurance policy—a policy my family would have given anything not to have collected. Yet money is a form of power; it allows for possibilities otherwise unfathomable. How do we reconcile these often-contradictory realities?

I knew it wasn't enough to just leave my family a fat inheritance. If you've lost someone close to you, you don't need me to tell you that I'd have traded in all my college money for just a little more time with my father.

Over the next few years, I started to rebuild my sense of self brick by brick. I began by asking myself some uncomfortable questions. Who am I outside of being a doctor? What makes my life feel purposeful? What do I consider "enough"—and how does money play into that? What would I most want to do even if I weren't getting paid to do it? When do I feel most at peace? Most myself? And, just as important, what do I want to accomplish on this earth before I die, and what is keeping me from doing it now?

As I started to answer these questions, I was able to peel away the parts of being a doctor that no longer fit. I left my concierge practice and spent more time doing the one thing that still felt authentic and good about medicine: hospice and palliative care.

Obviously this work was deeply connected to the loss I'd experienced so young, but no more was I a kid in an oversized lab coat playing the role of my father. This was work I felt uniquely suited for, work that I wanted to do no matter what it paid.

This work also informed my burgeoning "second career" as a financial expert. That was a career path I never really planned for but that took shape quite naturally when I started speaking and writing about what I felt most passionate about. In caring for the dying and their families, I found myself receiving answers to so many questions I'd been grappling with for years, from distinguishing my own goals and dreams from those of my father to understanding the role money played in my life. In fact, the more patients I interacted with, the more it became clear that the dying have much to teach about money and life.

The phrase "We're dying from the moment we're born" is so often repeated that it's become a cliché. But how often is that knowledge hiding just underneath the surface of our conscious thought and behavior, pushing our buttons in ways we don't always see? Certainly the loss of my father and my anxiety around my own mortality drove me forward for much of my life, and yet it took me decades to understand how central my fear of death was when it came to the story I was telling about my identity, my calling, and my sense of safety and security.

Perhaps you have your own story that's helped you make sense of the uncertainty of life and inevitability of death. What stories are you telling yourself right now about why you do the work you do? About how you spend your "free time"? About what money means or doesn't mean to you?

Have these stories been affecting the way you spend money on yourself and your family? Have they been influencing how many hours you work each week and how much you allow yourself to indulge in your hobbies or passions? Are any of these stories connected with early losses or traumas? If so, is it possible that these stories need to be examined more deeply?

Every patient I've ever sat down with has their own versions of these stories. But when a person is diagnosed with a terminal illness and death goes from a feared possibility to a certainty, something remarkable frequently happens: often those self-protective stories about identity, work, and money crumble, leaving a person with great clarity about who they are, what they love, and what really matters.

That doesn't mean a terminal diagnosis is ever easy—not for the patients, their loved ones, or their caregivers. But what I have observed is that for a lot of people, the understanding that death is near gives as well as takes: When death becomes certain, it's like a vise grip around the neck has been loosened. Focus shifts away from a fear of loss and toward the possibility of what can still be gained and experienced.

Often, people begin to focus on their true desires for the first time.

When I told one of my chronically ill patients, Sam, that he was dying and nothing more could be done, he paused before speaking. Finally, he said, "But, Doc, I don't have time for this right now!"

He then burst into a loud spasm of laughter. His girlfriend couldn't turn back the smile that fought through her tears.

This wasn't the only bright memory I have of Sam. As soon as he got the diagnosis, something shifted in him. He no longer had to fret over whether he was going to die or not—because the diagnosis left little room for doubt.

There was also little time to waste. Throughout his life, he had constantly put off his wish to be spontaneous and see the world. He always had an excuse not to pursue his frivolous wishes and dreams. But he no longer had to play it safe. And so when we would call Sam over the next few months to set up his next appointment, he was rarely at home.

"He's in New Orleans," his daughter told me one time when I made a call myself. "He went to Mardi Gras!"

Sam took many other trips in the months after receiving his diagnosis. One afternoon, his girlfriend came to check on him and found him lying in bed peacefully. When she realized he was no longer breathing, she reached for the phone to call the hospice nurse. That's when she noticed a single suitcase next to the foot of the bed. She opened it to find that Sam had packed his favorite suit, his lucky shirt, and a brand-new pair of shoes. This was odd, since they hadn't planned any more trips.

As I hung up the phone, I realized that Sam was sending us all a message. To him, death was just another adventure. And he wanted to make sure his bag was packed.

What if we all could begin to live like Sam not simply during our final days, but *every* day?

The more I began to learn from my patients, the less certain I was about a lot of my ideas concerning frugality, saving, and investing. Post in any financial independence forum or Facebook group about a big purchase, and the dissenting opinions come quickly. Over and over again, the claim is that by spending on these big-ticket items, we incur an "opportunity cost." In other words, if we had invested the money instead, it would "compound" exponentially, making it possible for us to enjoy much more opportunity in the future.

Compounding, most simply explained, is the exponential growth of an interest-bearing investment. You could say that it is the interest that you earn off your interest. Any financial text worth its salt will describe in great detailed mathematical terms how small sums of money allowed to grow with compound interest will become large sums of money over ever-expanding periods of time. All you have to do is sit back, relax, and wait for the money to grow.

But here's what my time with people like Sam drove home: money isn't the only thing that compounds. Experience compounds. The time and energy we put into our relationships and explorations of the world compounds. Education compounds, as does joy.

At the beginning of my career, my sister and her husband moved to Australia for a year for a temporary job relocation. Burdened by our busy careers and leftover college debt, my wife and I decided to save instead of visiting them. Years later, I have huge regrets about not taking the trip. Of course, the thousands of dollars that we didn't spend may have compounded into tens of thousands of dollars now. I could easily afford the trip today. But I can never go back and rewrite myself into that youthful adventure. And we mustn't forget the true value of things.

My association with the FIRE movement has deepened my understanding of my financial needs and allowed me to build a stable plan and free myself from unsatisfying work. Yet working with the dying also helped me see that the foundations of the movement are steeped in fear: fear of not having enough money; fear of working away at a job that is unfulfilling; and, perhaps most of all, fear of dying broke.

Such fears can not only drive extreme behavior when it comes to frugality, career choices, and deprivation, but also lead to confusion about meaning and purpose. This is something I learned from my patients, too; the lessons I received from the dying were not always positive.

Liz was in her early forties when she discovered the personal finance world. Enthralled by the prospect of financial independence and building a life of abundance for her two young children, she set off on a plan to stabilize the family budget. She worked dutifully on saving and investing, and within a few years, she was well on the road to financial independence.

Liz's joy about her newfound financial security, however, was short-lived. She found herself restless and uncertain. Instead of feeling elated, she began struggling with depression. Now that her money issues were managed, she didn't know where to focus her energy. She lost the drive to spend more hours in the office in the pursuit of a goal that was now all but certain.

The mirage of wealth had obscured the fact that money is a tool, not a goal. Attaining that goal had left a vacuum that Liz didn't know how to fill. As she became more and more depressed, she lost focus. She spent more time abusing alcohol and less time sleeping. It was only a matter of time before tragedy struck. They say she fell asleep at the wheel.

I met Liz and her family only briefly before the family decided to remove her life support. The car accident had caused irreversible brain damage, and it was unlikely that Liz would ever awaken again. A few days after sitting with her husband, Carl, and comforting him while the respirator was being removed, I called him at home to see how he was doing. His voice cracked as he pondered his unbearable feelings of loss and shared more about Liz's last days.

"Liz had been so concerned with money at the end," he told me. "I would have gladly worked night and day for the rest of my life to just have another year with her!"

While I have met other patients and families who have expressed similar regret, I have also watched those who, upon being diagnosed with a terminal illness, embrace their time left on this earth in ways that might surprise people who long for early retirement.

Bobbie was obsessed with trucks from a young age. He dreamed about one day having a big rig of his own. He parlayed his childhood fantasies into a booming business buying and selling the gargantuan vehicles he'd fallen in love with as a kid. Every morning, he would pace back and forth in the lot admiring his beauties before settling down to his desk and beginning the endless process of matching buyers and sellers.

Once a booming business, by the time of his passing, the entity was mostly devoid of value. Although his customer base had dried up, Bobbie still loved what work remained. As his congestive heart failure progressed, I would visit him in his shop. His assistant had placed Bobbie's recliner in close proximity to his desk so he could peruse the sales sheets in between dozing off throughout the day. His body was giving in, but not his excitement for the deal.

Now, a lot of conventional wisdom would say that Bobbie should have set things up so he could have stepped away from his career a lot earlier. But, I assure you, there is nowhere on earth that man wanted to be more than his shop.

Bit by bit, my experiences as a hospice doctor have not only transformed the story that a grieving seven-year-old once told himself; they've also changed the way I think about how I spend my time and what I truly value. They've helped me weed out a lot of financial advice some view as sacred, because what's liberating for one person can be torture for another.

Perhaps the biggest lesson has been what elaborate lengths we go through in our attempts to shield ourselves from our mortality. Sometimes our fears of dying mean we play it safe or follow a path that's not our own. Other times we become so enamored by the mirage of wealth that we spend our lives chasing some elusive goal that doesn't really exist. For many of us, it is only when we find out that we are dying or terminally ill that the illusion shatters.

What a gift it would be to start at the beginning as opposed to the end of our journey—to learn to live before it's too late. Wealth and financial know-how should not come at the expense of honoring what's important to us; quite the contrary—they should be our boons on this most important journey of living.

This book is a celebration of all that my patients have taught me about living and dying. The book is a critical look at the conventional wisdom so many of my peers swear by when it comes to the complicated relationship between money and life.

But the wisdom I've gained from the dying goes much deeper than throwing fiscal responsibility out the window because "YOLO" (you only live once). In fact, the way I see it, we *don't* only live once. We live countless lives as well as suffer pain and loss over and over again. Each graduation or career milestone, each disappointment or heartbreak can feel like the end of one life and the beginning of another. As a hospice doctor, I find it more accurate to say that we only die once!

While nothing is permanent, for some people, it's only when they face their own impending nonexistence that they begin to openly and honestly evaluate their life. The certainty of death removes the fears and barriers that have paralyzed us from asking the important questions. There is no time left to hesitate. Who do we want to be? What do we value? How important is money, and what are we willing to sacrifice for it?

The answers to these questions are instrumental in filling the oft-ignored holes that exist within when it comes to our identities and purpose. Such gaps must be filled in preparation for a "good" death. It is a time to mend relationships, fix that which has been broken, and fulfill last-minute "bucket list" items. The end is both a gift and a hardship.

The gift of mortality, however, becomes even more powerful in the hands of those who are not imminently facing death. There is no reason we can't use everyday loss and suffering to give us the courage to start asking questions about identity and purpose today. Loss is always around the corner. The old cliché rings true: *We should learn to live as if we are dying.*

The problem is that the future is uncertain. We don't know whether we will die tomorrow or in a few decades. That's why it's not enough to just follow principles or rules that others have put forth about wise wealth management and financial investment. Dealing with money effectively will always involve more than just balancing income and outflow and more than budgeting and saving. Our goal is to put our finances "on autopilot" so our money is working for us—but that is not the same thing as being on autopilot ourselves.

The stories, ideas, and framework I'll share in the pages to come will drive home the most important lessons I've learned from my patients and my own life. The chapters to come will remind us that wealth is just a lever, and that *real* wealth goes far beyond money. By asking the right questions, we can use this tool to rewrite the outdated stories we tell ourselves that are no longer self-affirming.

Too many people look to financial advisers to tell them exactly what to do. What these people really need is to have a better understanding of who they are and what they want to accomplish. When this valuable lesson from the dying is taken into account, personal decisions about money management become crystal clear. My goal in writing this book is to use this knowledge to help you build a financial plan free of clichés and oversimplistic catchphrases. My goal is to help you build a legacy that is uniquely yours.

CHAPTER 1

MONEY IS LIKE OXYGEN

TWO STORIES OF DYING IN AMERICA

After years of walking among the dying I have come to one overwhelming conclusion: we are scared to death—of dying. Studies show that a significant portion of people are afraid of death and the deaths of their loved ones. In fact, there is even a field of study devoted to the human reaction to death and dying: thanatology.

But just as pervasive is our fear of *life*. Specifically, we're afraid of screwing up our one shot to live a good life. This fear pervades just about everything we do, leading to shame and disappointment and straining our relationships. We set standards high, then obsess about what will happen if we fall short.

All too often, these standards are built on a rocky foundation of ideas we've never really examined. Central among them is the belief that if we just accumulate *enough* wealth, it will somehow stave off death or at least mitigate our inadequacies and disappointments. No wonder there is a mental health crisis! We can't escape death. We can't control it. We can throw all the money at death that we want, but no amount can keep it away forever.

I want to share two stories of people living, and dying, under very different economic circumstances. On the surface, they share little more than a close proximity to death. But if we can look past their bank accounts, we'll see two men who died with the same regret: that they did not have enough.

CHARLIE'S STORY

Signing the divorce papers was probably Charlie's lowest point. His wife was sitting by his side, occasionally swatting at some fly buzzing around the room.

There was no fly.

Charlie tried to focus on the legal papers through his tears. He had no intention of leaving his beloved's side. But to ensure Paula received an adequate level of care for her Alzheimer's, he had to sign the divorce papers and declare her bankrupt. Only then would Medicaid pay.

He regretted not being able to take Paula home to live out her final days— although one could barely call the cramped condo they'd been forced to downsize to years earlier a "home." Their last days together bore little resemblance to the years they'd spent raising their kids in a tony suburb. More than anything, Charlie regretted how little they'd thought about their financial future when there was still time.

Charlie's health deteriorated rapidly after Paula's death. He used what little energy he had to clear out his best friend's belongings from the tiny space they shared. Any last bit of money the divorce had spared was gone. His body was weak, his joints stiff. He got into bed one evening after drinking a little too much and, when he woke up, found he lacked the strength to lift himself up. Instead, he gently rolled down to the floor and crawled into the bathroom. There would be no 911 calls. He would not spend his last days in some godforsaken institution. It was bad enough admitting to his kids that he needed help; he cherished his time with them and didn't want them to know how tight things had gotten.

Eventually, Charlie's heart failed. His doctor recommended immediate hospitalization. Charlie refused. When the doctor pleaded with him to hire around-the-clock caregivers, Charlie laughed. He barely could keep his lights on and the water running with his measly Social Security checks.

Charlie died with his kids at his side and a heart full of love, memories, and experiences—but with a bank account devoid of the funds needed to provide the most basic comfort.

CONNOR'S STORY

Connor vaguely heard his grandfather's words while adding the last flourishes to an email. Something about working too much—about none of his money being worth the sacrifice. Connor's quick glance at his Rolex confirmed that his sister would arrive in a few minutes to take over the babysitting obligation. His meeting with the distributors could be delayed only so long.

He turned to his grandfather. "Come on, Grandpa, you pretty much own this hospital wing!"

The patriarch was dying. He began building a multibillion-dollar manufacturing business when he was Connor's age, and now here he was, about to leave his legacy to his thankless children and his self-absorbed grandchildren. Connor, his namesake, was no better than the rest. Yet what could he expect? The young man shared much more than his name. His tenacity and focus made him a perfect fit to take the helm of the multinational conglomerate.

For his part, Connor respected his grandfather—even revered him. But the old man's passing at the hands of some cancer or another was neither sad nor surprising. It was just another inconvenience in the busy life of a young CEO.

When Connor finally took his eyes off his phone, it was too late. His grandfather had stopped breathing. Some great force had mysteriously extinguished itself.

I wonder what might have gone through Connor's head at this moment. Was he thinking about his own work not being worth it? About what his own wife was doing those nights he was away on business?

Is that what his grandfather was talking about?

The alarm on Connor's iPhone buzzed: the meeting was in fifteen minutes. He tucked his briefcase under his arm and rushed past the nursing station toward the elevator. It never occurred to him to notify his family.

The patriarch was dead.

WHEN ENOUGH IS NOT ENOUGH

Why, despite such radically different circumstances, do these stories share such a similar sense of tragedy? Charlie had an enviable relationship with his wife and clearly loved her until the last moment. But without enough money, he was stuck with few choices, a "Medicaid" divorce, and a shocking lack of comfort as he lay dying.

Connor Sr., a powerful businessman who could buy his own hospital wing, had different regrets. His daily activities lacked purpose. His identity was wholly defined by his work. He died without experiencing love or true connection.

He found that "more than enough" was also not enough.

In 2019, I had the opportunity to interview Jim Dahle, the creator of *The White Coat Investor*, a platform for high-income professionals to get a "fair shake" on Wall Street. We were having a discussion about wealth, happiness, and the correlation between them.

When some of our listeners expressed the opinion that most of our struggles are about something "deeper than money," Jim was incredulous.

"I think it is easy to get on our high horse when you're already financially independent and sit there and say that money doesn't matter," he said. "But guess what? If there is nothing in the bank account and your kid is hungry or you need to go down to see the doctor or the car just dropped its transmission—you know what? Money matters a lot!"

That day, he compared money to oxygen. If you have enough, it doesn't affect your life all that much. But if you don't have enough, good luck thinking about anything else!

I remember his words hit me like a ton of bricks. They helped me understand I'd previously held a very privileged position on personal finance. For so long I had been underplaying the importance of material wealth because I had "graduated from basic sustenance." I was doing my best to "embrace the abundance mindset" and "escape scarcity thinking."

And yet I had failed to grasp a fundamental truth: only when our basic economic needs are met do we have the luxury to say that "money doesn't matter."

The data bears out the wrongheadedness of the way I had been thinking. In 2017, a survey by Bankrate showed that of 1,003 people surveyed, 57 percent didn't have enough cash to cover an unexpected $500 expense.[1] And this was before the economy and job market were decimated by the COVID-19 pandemic.

In August 2020, according to a bimonthly survey by the technology company SimplyWise, 38 percent of people who had lost a job or had their income reduced due to COVID-19 couldn't survive a month with savings of any kind.[2] Even more alarming, one in five couldn't last two weeks off their savings, emergency fund, or money earmarked for retirement. A good deal of our population is one tragedy, lost job, or mistake away from poverty.

As these statistics reveal, we are in the midst of an economic crisis that cannot be chalked up to individual behavior alone. And so those of us still trying to get on steady ground should feel no shame about the journey ahead. While this book is not explicitly focused on getting out of debt, it is filled with practical financial basics we all need to know—and, more important, the mindsets that can help us understand what money really is and how to use it wisely.

---

1   Bankrate, "Nearly 60% of Americans Can't Afford Common Unexpected Expenses," *January Money Pulse*, January 12, 2017, https://www.bankrate.com/pdfs /pr/20170112-January-Money-Pulse.pdf.
2   Greg Iacurci, "Nearly 40% of Cash-Strapped Americans Can't Last a Month on Savings," CNBC, August 19, 2020, https://www.cnbc.com/2020/08/19/nearly -40percent-of-cash-strapped-americans-cant-last-a-month-on-savings.html.

What's more, those of us who have the luxury of not having to stress about basic needs shouldn't be so quick to congratulate ourselves. Let's take the oxygen metaphor a step further to understand why. If life is not possible without at least a certain level of oxygen for comfort, what happens when you have excess? Does extra oxygen get you anywhere? Do you develop superhuman strength, live longer, or even feel better?

While some may argue the answer, I can tell you without a doubt as a physician that there is nothing gained by having more oxygen than your lungs and body need to survive. In fact, at very high levels, oxygen is likely toxic and causes damage to the lungs and heart.

So why don't we realize the same truth about money? Why do we chase higher and higher amounts, when we have by far surpassed "enough"? Furthermore, why do we feel that after getting our basic needs met, more money will somehow lead us to greater self-fulfillment or self-actualization?

I call this kind of thinking the "fallacy of enough"—this idea that, once we reach some sort of plateau (whether wealth, achievement, or happiness), a great calm will overcome us. In reality, I have found that once we reach our goals, fear sets in. We immediately start to worry we will lose everything we worked so hard to gain in the first place, and the sheer terror can greatly outshine the pleasure of the accomplishment.

You may be familiar with the cognitive bias known as *loss aversion*, an idea coined by psychologists Amos Tversky and Daniel Kahneman.[3] To put the concept in its simplest terms, the pain of losing is psychologically twice as powerful as the pleasure of gaining. And so we'll go to incredible lengths to avoid the loss that scares us so much. Perhaps that's why whenever we reach a place we'd once believed was enough, we become terrified of falling. We start chasing the next goal before we even celebrate reaching this one.

---

3   D. Kahneman and A. Tversky, "Prospect Theory: An Analysis of Decision under Risk," *Econometrica* 47, no. 4 (1979): 263–291.

Our brains seem hardwired to never be satisfied. Or worse yet, they trick us into thinking that real gains or accomplishments pale in comparison to how much worse off we'll be if we lose what we have.

So are we doomed?

Is "enough" just an illusion?

FLATTENING MASLOW'S PYRAMID

A great place to begin our "journey to enough" is at the base of a famous pyramid with which you may be familiar.

In his 1943 paper "A Theory of Human Motivation," Abraham Maslow, a renowned psychologist, introduced his hierarchy of needs to help clarify what drives human motivation.[4] At the lowest levels are our basic physiologic requirements: food, water, warmth, safety. As one scales to the top, however, the more ephemeral needs become dominant: love, prestige, creativity, and achieving one's purpose (figure 1).

Figure 1. Maslow's pyramid

It takes only a glance to remember what Jim Dahle reminded me of when we spoke: "enough" requires our basic safety and physiologic needs to

---

4 A. H. Maslow, "A Theory of Human Motivation," *Psychological Review* 50, no. 4 (1943): 430–437.

be met. Money (food, water, safety) is like oxygen; it is pretty darn near impossible to live without it.

But when I think about what I've learned from patients like Connor Sr., I view the pyramid a little differently. Should we envision each stage in the pyramid as a step we must master before climbing to the higher, "more complicated" strata? Do belonging, esteem, and fulfillment all depend on surpassing the first two levels? Traditional teaching tells us this is the case. But I think it's time we flatten Maslow's pyramid.

Look no further than the two stories at the beginning of this chapter. There is no question that Connor Sr. had long surpassed the basic needs steps of the pyramid. Yet at the end of his life, he was nowhere near the top of the triangle of self-fulfillment. There was no love in his life, no deep relationships. He had failed to progress.

Charlie, on the other hand, lived with an abundance of love and relationships. He climbed the triangle even while struggling financially. Money might have been scarce, but he navigated his life with meaning and purpose.

Did Charlie "break" the pyramid? Did the patriarch? Or have we learned that, more likely, a hierarchical layering of needs is in fact unrealistic? The path to enough should look less like climbing a pyramid and more like circling a twisting spiral, always making sure we don't neglect one key area in favor of another.

A lack of money will no more hold one back from a sense of self-esteem or self-actualization than owning a multibillion-dollar company will provide one. You don't have to reach one level in order to climb to the next. Instead, it's a big messy hodgepodge, with your average person meeting some of their needs and not others, and the most fulfilled among us keeping all five areas in mind.

While it is fairly easy to read Charlie's story and understand what was lacking, many of us are perplexed by stories like Connor Sr.'s. Why hadn't he progressed past basic needs when he had so much?

I have taken care of many patients like Connor Sr. in my career. I have watched them stumble from achievement to achievement and monetary goal to monetary goal. They find contentment elusive. Their happiness is short-lived; it comes and goes with each achievement.

Why?

OVERDRIVE

Almost any book you read about personal finance will at some point talk about a concept called the "hedonic treadmill."

We all lust after fancy shiny objects from time to time: cars, jewelry, houses, you name it. And indeed, a fresh purchase often pushes our momentary sense of happiness through the roof.

We marvel at the exquisite beauty parked in our driveway or how the rock shimmers on our finger. Yet, with the passage of time, we return to our baseline. (See figure 2.) We are no happier—probably just a little more broke.

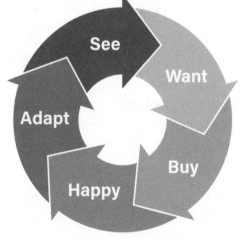

Figure 2. The hedonic treadmill

There's a reason for that, provided by a theory known as "the hedonic treadmill." In brief, it holds that human beings are able to adapt to changes so quickly that we tend to stay at a basic level of happiness no matter what positive or negative life changes we experience. That's why our purchases bring us a sense of short-term well-being that disappears almost instantaneously: we adapt. Before we know it, we're online searching for the next thing to buy, hoping to re-create that momentary sense of happiness.

Why? Because it's human nature. Because consumption is addictive. That's why it's called a treadmill. Our legs are moving faster and faster, but, in reality, we're getting nowhere. The hedonic treadmill is the reason many of us find ourselves having to make the same impossible end-of-life decisions as Charlie.

What many financial experts fail to warn us about, however, is that there is a twin cousin to the hedonic treadmill that is every bit as devastating. I like to call it *overdrive*, and it is especially common in those who are drawn to the idea of financial independence. For many of us, saving and making money, not spending it, gives us momentary bumps of happiness—those addictive little hits of dopamine.

The problem is that, just as with the regular hedonic treadmill, our money wins do not permanently elevate happiness. Whenever the shine of that new milestone fades, we're back to our baseline—which sends us off to the races to try to make even more money.

When I talk of overdrive, I'm not talking about that gear setting on your car that no one understands. But let's stick with the car metaphor: What happens when the wheels are moving, but the car is jacked up and not touching the ground? You can put the pedal to the metal and increase the spin as much as you want. The car still isn't moving.

Ah, but I hear your objections: the hedonic treadmill is a great theory and all, but when it comes to money, more indeed does buy greater happiness. Once you can afford the finer things, life becomes infinitely easier.

Let's look at the evidence.

DOES MORE MONEY BRING MORE HAPPINESS?

To understand the complex relationship between money and contentedness, we have to first explore the terms researchers use when studying such things. The two concepts that appear over and over again in these analyses are *emotional well-being* and *life evaluation*.

You may have heard of the 2010 Daniel Kahneman and Angus Deaton study of the effects of income on our lives.[5] When they measured the emotional well-being and the life evaluation of a thousand US residents, they found happiness increased up to an annual income of $75,000, but after that, the effect was negligible.

To study this concept further, in 2018, researchers in Purdue University's Department of Psychological Sciences looked at data from the Gallup World Poll, which is a representative survey sample of more than 1.7 million individuals from 164 countries.[6] The researchers found that money no longer effects emotional well-being after people reached an annual income of $60,000 to $75,000. The ideal income point for life evaluation was $95,000.

Interestingly enough, the study also found that once these income thresholds were reached, increased income tended to be associated with reduced life satisfaction or a reduced sense of day-to-day well-being. The authors of the study hypothesized that once these pivotal points are surpassed, people are driven to an increase in material consumerism and peer comparisons that often have an overall negative impact. Sounds a little like overdrive, doesn't it?

---

5   D. Kahneman and A. Deaton, "High Income Improves Evaluation of Life but Not Emotional Well-Being," *Proceedings of the National Academy of Sciences of the United States of America* 107, no. 38 (2010): 16489–16493, doi: 10.1073/pnas.10114 92107.

6   A. T. Jebb, L. Tay, E. Diener, and S. Oishi, "Happiness, Income Satiation, and Turning Points around the World," *Nature Human Behaviour* 2 (2018), 33–38.

Newer research in 2021 by Matthew Killingsworth questions the conclusions of the 2010 study by Kahneman and Deaton.[7] Although Killingsworth found that money correlates with happiness past the $75,000 threshold, the association is quite small and is mostly driven by those who believe that money matters to them.

I GOT IT ALL WRONG

I can write confidently about overdrive because I've been a victim of it myself. For much of my adult life, I had far more than enough but kept thinking that if I just made more, I would be happier. If my salary were bigger. If my net worth were higher. If my 401(k) were growing faster.

But there is no prize for having more than enough. In fact, there are penalties. My voyage to wealth was sucking up my time, my energy, and often my goodwill. My children grew, my parents aged, my siblings built families around me.

And I was busy—often too busy to spend time with any of them.

Why? Why do we get so confused? Why do we miss the importance and value of all the nonmonetary things in our lives and replace them with goals of wealth and materialism?

Further complicating matters is the fact that American culture (as well as that of many other modern-day societies) encourages our behavior. Our culture promotes workaholism, consumerism, and a general culture of keeping up with the Joneses. We are obsessed with buying the newest, latest, and greatest. Once they are purchased, we display our things and lifestyle proudly for the rest of the world to see and admire.

Don't believe me? Let's look at the facts. In 2014, a Gallup poll showed that Americans work more hours per week than most developed coun-

---

7   M. Killingsworth, "Experienced Well-Being Rises with Income, Even Above $75,000 Per Year," *PNAS* 118, no. 4 (January 26, 2021): e2016976118, doi: 10.1073/pnas.2016976118.

tries.[8] The actual number was forty-seven hours, significantly more than in countries like Germany and Sweden, where people's weekly work hours were closer to thirty-five.

Americans also tend to shun vacation to a greater extent than citizens of other countries. A grassroots movement, Project Time Off, studied this phenomenon in 2017 and found that 52 percent of employed Americans left some of their vacation time on the table.[9] And remember, unlike most countries, in the United States as little as two weeks a year of vacation is considered standard. The data when it comes to nights and weekends is even worse (figure 3).

Americans Work Nights And Weekends The Most

Percent of workers in the United States working nights and weekends*

■ Weekend Work   ■ Night Work

	United States	United Kingdom	Germany	France	Netherlands
Weekend Work	29.2%	25.5%	22.4%	21.8%	
Night Work	26.6%	18.6%	12.0%	7.2%	18.7% / 6.9%

ⓒⓘ⊜
@StatistaCharts

* Most recent figures available
Source: Hamermesh and Stancanelli

statista ◢

Figure 3. Comparing night and weekend work habits between countries[10]

---

8   Lydia Saad, "The '40 Hour' Work Week Is Actually Longer—by Seven Hours," *Gallup*, August 29, 2014, https://news.gallup.com/poll/175286/hour-workweek-actually-longer-seven-hours.aspx.

9   Megan Leonhardt, "Only 28% of Americans Plan to Max Out Their Vacation Days This Year," *CNBC Make It*, April 27, 2019, https://www.cnbc.com/2019/04/26/only-28percent-of-americans-plan-to-max-out-their-vacation-days-this-year.html.

10   Statista, "Americans Work Nights and Weekends the Most," October 10, 2014, https://www.statista.com/chart/2812/americans-work-nights-and-weekends-the-most.

We not only lead in the number of off-hours activities, but also a full quarter of Americans work at least some nights and weekends.

The data, of course, begs the simple question: Why? Is it that we love our jobs so much? Not according to a Gallup poll in 2019 that surveyed 6,633 working adults to assess their job satisfaction.[11] The poll found that only 40 percent of American workers surveyed considered themselves to be in "good jobs," compared to 16 percent of the workforce who believe they're in "bad jobs." The remaining 44 percent of workers say they are in "mediocre jobs."

These numbers are abysmal!

In summary, we are working harder than ever, skipping vacation, and filling up nights and weekends for jobs that we for the most part find at best mediocre or possibly poor. Why, oh why, do we do this to ourselves? Why do we trade our most precious commodity, time, for this unhappy scenario?

Could the reason be fear?

WHY ARE WE SO STRESSED?

Money is the biggest source of stress for Americans, research shows. Indeed, a 2018 survey by Northwestern Mutual found that money was the dominant source of stress for 44 percent of Americans (144 million), followed by personal relationships (25 percent), with just 18 percent blaming work.[12] Data from the American Psychological Association also shows that money is the number one stressor for Americans: "Regard-

---

11   Megan Henney, "Most American Workers Don't Like Their Job, Study Finds," *Fox Business*, October 24, 2019, https://www.foxbusiness.com/markets/american -job-satisfaction-gallup-poll.

12   Northwestern Mutual, "Planning and Progress Study 2018," March 19, 2018, https://news.northwesternmutual.com/planning-and-progress-2018.

less of the economic climate, money and finances have remained the top stressor since our survey began in 2007."[13]

We can partly explain these fears using Maslow's theories. A significant percent of our population just doesn't have enough so they are stuck at the beginning levels of fulfilling their basic needs.

But this theory certainly doesn't explain people like Charlie, who climbed to the so-called top levels without having basic needs addressed. It doesn't explain why I languished in my profession far past the point of enjoyment and well into serious burnout. And it flies in the face of evidence that a good portion of middle- and upper-class America has enough to survive and yet finds their day-to-day employment a cause of a great deal of chronic stress and distress.

The answer is simple, and it is right there in front of our faces. We are looking to money to do what it was never designed to do! Wealth has transitioned from a tool into a goal. We think if we just make enough money, it will somehow turn us into good people, solve our day-to-day problems, or better yet help us cope with that great fear: that we will come to the end of life without enough.

It's much easier to put off such difficult thoughts and leave them for another day.

But what if we quit putting those thoughts off?

What if we faced our fear of death head-on?

What if we defined what "enough" really looks like so that we could pursue that goal with clarity and purpose?

---

13   American Psychological Association, "American Psychological Association Survey Shows Money Stress Weighing on Americans' Health Nationwide," press release, February 2015, https://www.apa.org/news/press/releases/2015/02/money -stress.

REDEFINING "ENOUGH"
WITH LIFE REVIEW

There is very little that is enviable about receiving a terminal diagnosis. For many, it is the worst moment in their lives. I have had this conversation over and over again in some of the most agonizing circumstances. Yet, after the initial shock dies down, a much deeper, richer period of self-evaluation and introspection often ensues. We call this process life review.

Life review is a holistic and structured process of evaluating one's past and present, including events and memories, in an attempt to find meaning in and achieve resolution of one's life. Often what happens is that a hospice caregiver or chaplain will sit down with a person and ask them to look back at their life. The caregiver will ask questions such as these: Which accomplishments am I proud of? Have I nurtured my relationships? Is there anything I regret?

These questions can be difficult and distressing at first. My patient Sheila and I spent quite a bit of time talking about her first marriage. She clearly remembers the day she walked into her bedroom and found her husband with a stranger. It was just months after their second miscarriage, and she found her heart breaking all over again.

Her anger was so intense that she picked up the phone and called a lawyer the very same day. Her divorce was swift and final. Without kids or economic attachments, she left the cozy apartment they shared and never turned back.

Decades later, dying in her late forties of leukemia, she regretted the impulsivity of her actions. Her pain had been so great that she was unable to connect with her husband about his pain. I was in the room the day she decided to call her ex-husband. After so many years of not talking, she wanted not only to forgive him, but also to take responsibility for her own actions. Making amends with this important but distant person in her life provided much comfort in her last days.

Sometimes life review helps us understand that "enough" really can be about money. Although Gertrude was in her eighties and dying from emphysema, she would always be a child of the Depression. The recollections of hunger were so profound that she often kept money hidden in different places throughout her house in case hard times hit unexpectedly. As her economic fortunes improved over time, Gertrude transferred those fears to her grandchildren. Their basic needs were taken care of, but would they have enough to go on vacation, or to college, or to build a life of their dreams?

Upon conducting a life review with the hospice team chaplain, Gertrude's fears came to the forefront as a major obstacle to dying a "good" death. Based on this knowledge, Gertrude's children decided to share their financial statements with their mother in an effort to quell her worries. When she saw how much was saved up in each of her grandchildren's 529 college funds, she felt a huge burden being lifted.

For many people, a life review is the only time they will ever pinpoint the areas where they fall short of "enough" and attempt to fill the gaps. So why do we wait for the diagnosis of a terminal illness to conduct such an important activity? What if we had the courage to do a life review now, well before the end is within sight? At the end of the chapter, I will provide some basic questions to ask yourself to assess where you're falling short when it comes to Maslow's needs.

But first, let's take what we've learned about the mind and motivation to understand how we can feel a sense of contentment even when we're falling a little short.

THE CLIMB

The best way to overcome the "fallacy of enough" is to change our relationship to "the climb." We can think of the climb as consistent progress toward a meaningful goal. That's it—no more or less.

Humans really do seem to need some kind of climb. We feel the most fulfilled and the closest to self-actualization not when we buy a new toy or reap the rewards of a great investment, but rather when we are doing purposeful things and aspiring to something of great personal meaning.

Maslow called this stage of development self-actualization. Happiness researchers use the terms "emotional well-being" and "life evaluation." In her classic book *The Top Five Regrets of the Dying*, Bronnie Ware describes how her patients wished that they had lived a life "truer to themselves," not the life others expected of them.[14]

I call it the climb—more specifically, striving toward our own unique purpose, identity, and connections.

We should not approach the climb as a race. As a podcast guest of mine, Meyer Feldberg, lamented in his memoir, "There is no finish line."[15] There is no goal, no reward at the end—just a series of roads ahead of us and a choice of which is to be taken.

The dying realize this innately. They take on the urgency of now because, for them, there is no long term to set goals for. "Enough" becomes "joy in the process." One day at a time, one step at a time, until there are no more.

We, too, can jump off the treadmills and begin the climb to what really matters.

Dying is easy. What's hard is learning how to live: learning how to avoid the traps of loss aversion and overdrive and figure out what motivates us from within.

And that brings us to Chapter 2.

---

14   Bronnie Ware, *The Top Five Regrets of the Dying: A Life Transformed by the Dearly Departing* (Carlsbad, CA: Hay House, 2012).

15   Meyer Feldberg, *No Finish Line: Lessons on Life and Career* (New York: Columbia Business School Publishing, May 5, 2020).

DEFINING "ENOUGH" BEFORE IT'S TOO LATE: THE LIFE REVIEW

1. Clear your schedule for an hour for two to three separate days over the next week. During that time, make sure all electronics are turned to silent, you are well-rested and fed, and you have found a quiet, comfortable place to concentrate.

2. Close your eyes and imagine that you have gone into the doctor's office for your annual physical and feel great. When your doctor walks in, you note that her face is a little more serious than usual. That's when she informs you that you have only one more year to live. The fear and panic take over. Maybe you begin to sweat a bit.

3. If you feel some anxiety arise while doing this exercise, know that it's natural. Taking several deep breaths can help it pass. Over time, the anxiety recedes, and a reassuring calm washes down your shoulders. Now that the timing of when you are going to die is no longer in question, what do you feel empowered to contemplate and question?

4. Make a list of all those things you feel would be important to do, experience, or achieve before you leave this earth. This can include the traditional bucket list items, but also think about the story of your life so far. What's missing?

5. Be specific here and ask yourself some important questions:

- What relationships in my life need repair?
- What lifelong goals have I yet to achieve?
- What deep needs have I not had the courage to fulfill?
- What have I denied myself because I was too afraid to spend money?
- Which places have I always wanted to go? What legacy do I want to leave for my family and friends?
- In what areas do I not yet have "enough"?

6. You'll notice that "enough" is not about a specific number. Not yet, anyway. In the next chapters, we'll explore how to use both fiscal and human capital as levers to get to "enough" sooner. For now, simply ask yourself where you don't have enough. And be generous with your answers.

Don't be afraid to tackle each concept on different days. Maybe the first hour is spent thinking about that moment in the doctor's office, the second hour asking those important questions, and the third hour exploring "enough."

CHAPTER 2

WORK DOESN'T STOP WHEN YOU RETIRE

I recently was exchanging emails with an *Earn & Invest* podcast listener about his recent struggles. Unlike many who are new to financial independence—who are busy concentrating on accumulation—Jason was having the exact opposite issue. His debt was paid off. He and his wife had stable W-2 employment. All investments were on autopilot, and the road to financial independence was in clear sight.

But...he was miserable. He had lost interest in his hobbies and friendships. It was a challenge even getting out of bed. He couldn't understand the sadness he felt given how well his life was going. It didn't help that everyone around him insisted that he should "quit complaining and enjoy life!"

As we discussed Jason's feelings, my mind raced back to Liz, the young car accident victim whom we met in the introduction to this book. Both found that their momentary joy upon reaching their financial goals was overtaken by a sense of gloom and depression. Instead of being energized, they felt lost and unable to reconnect with their previous sense of direction.

I panicked. I saw the destructive force the promise of money had played in Liz's life and desperately wanted to protect Jason from having the same outcome. Only after Liz had fallen into a coma had her family realized how debilitating it can be to mistake money for the ultimate goal.

And yet, despite its emotional consequences, this mistake is easy to make. In fact, don't we all do this? We are socially conditioned to place too much value on money even from a young age, when it definitely doesn't deserve to be on such a high pedestal. We should think of it more as just an intermediary, an IOU: potential energy that allows us to move toward our unique purpose, identity, and connections. It doesn't matter how many IOUs we've piled up. If we haven't figured out where to reallocate that energy, we will feel malaise just like Liz and Jason.

So how do we start the process of reallocation?

How do we help Jason avoid finding himself on his deathbed unfulfilled and disconnected? How do we move past the money mirage to understand a deeper sense of purpose?

The first step is to rethink how we talk about money. We sing the praises of early retirement but rarely define what that really means. After all, most of us will continue to work long after we cash our last paycheck. So, if our goal is true independence, we need to dispel the notion that we'll reach some magic moment when we never have to work again.

In this chapter, we're going to dive deep into what we're really talking about when we use the words "money," "work," "employment," and "retirement." By reframing our understanding of these concepts, we can stop chasing elusive goals and start identifying and clarifying the life we want to live today and tomorrow.

REDEFINING WORK

The modern-day FIRE movement gained momentum in the United States on the fumes of the Great Recession of 2008–09. Highly paid tech employees feeling the crunch of a recession and the disillusionment of stress-filled jobs were looking for an escape hatch. The solution was simple: earn, save, and invest enough to never have to work again.

"Let your money do the work for you!"

This rallying cry encompassed the zeitgeist of a generation. *Work* automatically became bad...the opposite of *freedom*. To escape this indentured servitude, many followed the financial advice of early FIRE enthusiasts such as Mr. Money Mustache—forty-seven-year-old Canadian blogger Pete Adeney, who retired from his job as a software engineer in 2005 at the age of thirty. These FIRE enthusiasts dutifully saved and invested until their bank accounts were overflowing with cash—a feat less strenuous than expected for highly paid young professionals.

TERMS

Financial independence is the status of having enough income to pay one's living expenses for the rest of one's life without having to be employed or dependent on others.

FI: financial independence

FIRE: financial independence, retire early

The nirvana these young retirees experienced, however, was fleeting. Faced with at least five more decades of life and viewing *work* as anathema, a lack of direction ensued. Like Jason and Liz, these people were fairly clear about what they didn't want to do but had no idea how to bring passion back into their lives. They were passionate about making money, but once they had *enough*, what was the point?

And even the idea of *doing it yourself*—something that seemed glamorous when trapped in a darkened cubicle in a dreary office building—became tiresome when reality set in. Many bothersome household chores that used to be offloaded on hired help suddenly were the purview of these early retirees. It's hard to pat yourself on the back for leaving an air-conditioned office doing something you vaguely disliked to retire to a life of cleaning toilets and mowing the lawn because the service is no longer in the budget.

Tony, a retired hospice patient dying of lung cancer, put it best. While conducting a life review, he told his nurse, "I left my long-standing job as a dishwasher at a restaurant to do what?"

His retirement years were spent cooking, cleaning, and—you guessed it—doing his own dishes at home. As death was nearing, he realized that maintaining his social connections at work had been giving his life meaning. But when planning for retirement, he hadn't considered the importance of those connections. He had become so enamored with the idea of retiring that he failed to realize that "washing dishes is washing dishes."

It didn't matter whether he was performing this chore for his boss at the restaurant or at home for himself. While the "work" was the same, his job not only provided a salary but also connected him with people he loved.

Tony and those early FIRE practitioners were essentially making the same mistake: they failed to understand the true meaning of work and the importance it plays in one's sense of well-being.

The nature of work is simple but generally misunderstood. Work is something that we do all our lives; it never stops, not even in retirement. At its most basic, work is an activity we do to create goods and services. This is true whether we are doing this work for ourselves or for others. When we are doing it for others, we call it *employment*. If Tony washes dishes at his restaurant every weeknight, he has provided a service to the restaurant owner. That owner can pay for Tony's service by either feeding him or providing, in return, some other essential good or service—such as money.

> **TERMS**
>
> **Work** consists of activities we do to create goods and services. Employment is the act of creating goods and services for another person or business, often in exchange for money.

At home, after eating dinner, Tony also used to wash dishes. Although this was still work, in this case, he provided a service for himself. In exchange for doing that work, Tony had clean dishes as well as the ability to forgo the necessity of employing someone else to do it for him.

Why do we naturally classify work we do for others as "bad" and work we do for ourselves as "good"? What if we had the power to see both activities as substantially the same? We could then better understand the nature of money.

MONEY IS AN INTERMEDIARY

The concept of money has also been broadly misunderstood. Money has no value in itself. It is an intermediary—a holder of goods and services. It is potential energy we collect when we perform work for other people. When I save up money, I am collecting an IOU that can be spent almost universally. After receiving his paycheck as a dishwasher, Tony used to go to the local convenience store and exchange his IOU for his weekly groceries. He transformed his work of doing dishes into an IOU from his employer in the form of money—an intermediary—which could then be exchanged for ice cream from the owner of the grocery store.

When making life decisions based on money—including, for example, retiring at a set net worth—we are simply relying on this intermediary as a goal instead of an instrument. We are rejoicing in this potential energy, this IOU, instead of thinking deeply about how to use this energy to fulfill our unique purpose, identity, and connections.

Is it surprising that Jason felt at a loss when he reached his financial goals? He had amassed a huge amount of potential energy but had no idea how to reallocate it. Tony, on the other hand, realized only as he got closer to his deathbed that he should have stayed at his job longer. He was doing work either way, but he felt a greater sense of companionship and connection before he retired. The extra money he collected from his employer could have paid for a house cleaner instead.

DROPPING "RETIRE EARLY"

While these new definitions of work and money make defining retirement much clearer, they also beg the question whether we should even bother. Retirement comes when you have saved enough of these IOUs so that you can cover your future needs for goods and services, minus those you are willing to provide for yourself. This is retirement, whether you continue to make money or not.

But isn't leaving employment the ultimate goal?

It wasn't for Tony. And it might not have been even for Jason or Liz.

We need to learn how to shift our perspective when it comes to this deeply ingrained assumption. Instead of just saving enough to leave employment, the goal should be to accumulate enough of these IOUs to allocate them in such a way as to maximize our precious time so that we can do things we really want to do, things that give our lives meaning.

Unfortunately, this perspective shift can come too late. Tony arrived at this important conclusion only when the specter of his own mortality forced him to. Tony's initial retirement goals were very much in line with the traditional FIRE philosophy. To the credit of the financial independence movement, it is evolving to understand these less-measurable goals. The "retire early" portion of the acronym is being dropped, and several subgenres being explored within the FIRE community are spurring a more thoughtful reallocation of our time and energy.

So that you can begin to consider these subgenres in the context of your own life, let's examine how the FIRE movement has begun to incorporate two subsets of financial independence, Slow FI and Coast FI.

SLOW FI

Jessica Lynn blogs about personal finance on her site *The Fioneers*. Back in 2019, Jessica coined the term "Slow FI." When she first discovered financial independence, she was living more of the YOLO lifestyle; she was by no means frugal! While she saw much that she liked in the movement, like others, she was concerned with the deprivation mentality. Her goal was to both learn how to spend in the moment but also plan for the long term. Eventually, she embraced an idea she called Slow FI.

TERMS

Slow FI involves using the incremental financial freedom that an individual gains along the journey to financial independence to live a happier and healthier life, do better work, and build strong relationships.

Slow FI eschews a fast path to financial independence by allowing us to use some of our potential energy now instead of waiting for some ill-defined moment in the future that might never come. Jessica built a stable financial foundation that allowed her to cut back at her unfulfilling job long before reaching financial independence and to pursue passion projects with the time she freed up.

TERMS

YOLO (you only live once), like "carpe diem," expresses the idea that you should seize the day and live life to the fullest regardless of cost.

While Jessica delayed her net worth goals, and ultimately, retirement, her quality of life increased greatly. She could spend more time doing things she loved. She could both defer gratification and also live her best life now. She could even keep some of the most enjoyable parts of the YOLO lifestyle. In fact, she just recently invested in a camper van and will spend tens of thousands of dollars to convert it into a mini home on wheels to slowly travel throughout the United States. This type of purchase would have been unthinkable just a few short years ago. To quote Jessica, "Slow FI enables unique lifestyle designs long before reaching full financial independence."

COAST FI

The main problem with financial independence is that often it feels like an unreachable goal. Calculating the amount of money necessary for the rest of your life is daunting. Often the numbers climb into the millions and feel so far away. The Coast FI movement arose for those who felt that they could no longer delay their current happiness and wanted to pursue their dreams.[16] But they wanted to do so responsibly.

---

16   Four Pillar Freedom, "What Is Coast FIRE?" June 10, 2019, https://fourpillarfreedom.com/what-is-coast-fire.

The Coast FI technique takes advantage of the adage that the best time to plant a tree is twenty years ago. As we have discussed, there is magic in the process of compounding. We can use that magic to start reaping the advantages of financial independence long before we get to the exact net worth necessary to support our lifestyle.

Coast FI is a form of reverse engineering. Using techniques we will discuss in Chapter 5, we can calculate the size of our future retirement nest egg. We can then use compounding and average investment returns to figure out how much money we need invested today to grow to that level. Although this sounds complicated, let's use some real numbers.

If you spend $40,000 a year to live comfortably, then you will need roughly a million dollars in invested assets to retire. Assuming you are thirty years old and want to retire at sixty-five, you have thirty-five years for your investments to compound. Based on an annual return of 5 percent (which is pretty conservative), you will need to invest $182,000 by the age of 30 to become a millionaire by the time you want to stop working.

Having that $182,000 does not make you suddenly financially independent, but investing and compounding will allow you to stop saving completely; all you have to do is make enough money each year to cover living expenses. The idea is to coast to financial independence over the next thirty-five years.

Both Slow FI and Coast FI will let you enjoy the benefits of financial independence long before you get there—having more control of the activities that fill your time. The earlier you start, the more powerful the effect of compound interest. If you start as early as your twenties, your wealth will grow exponentially.

Armed with our new definitions, we are able to see that Slow FI and Coast FI are both solutions to the deeper problem of understanding the dichotomy of money. It is the most important as well as the least important aspect of our lives.

But how can it be both?

MONEY IS A MIRAGE

Up to this point we have talked about money using various metaphors: an IOU, potential energy, a mirage. These terms are meant to signify that we often overemphasize the importance of money and the role it plays in our happiness. Jason and Liz are prime examples. They found that reaching their financial goals provided no more sense of contentedness or self-actualization. Tony, on the other hand, realized that being employed as a dishwasher was more fulfilling than retirement.

Why was he in such a rush to leave employment, then?

Remembering Maslow's flattened pyramid, we need money for the essentials, and yet money is not enough to provide a deeper sense of well-being and fulfillment. And more important, it is easy to concentrate on the concept of money and forget that it is a false goal. We get distracted by the mirage of money and the trancelike state that worshiping wealth induces, which I call the money mind meld.

When I say that money is a mirage, I'm classifying wealth as a false goal—an artificial endpoint that carries none of the joy that we associate with true accomplishment. Take a moment to consider the concept of a *bucket list*.

TERMS

A **bucket list** is a compilation of a number of experiences or achievements that a person hopes to have or accomplish during their lifetime.

You'll notice the words "experiences" and "achievements" are interchangeable with "goals." No one ever put a specific net worth in their bucket list; doing so would feel counterintuitive. It's not money that holds such import but rather what money allows us to do. As Gertrude Stein famously wrote in *Everybody's Autobiography* (1937), "There is no there there."[17]

---

17   Gertrude Stein, *Everybody's Autobiography* (New York: Random House, 1937).

So why do we pray to this false God?

Why do we abandon experiences and achievements in favor of our bank accounts?

Why do we think that if we just have enough money, everything will be better?

The answers to these questions were beginning to stir in my chest on that fateful day I discovered financial independence. It was the reason that I, like Jason and Liz, found my own financial success so disorienting and depressing. I had spent a lifetime focusing on money for the simple reason that it was easier, less stressful, and more accepted by friends and family than focusing on other, more unusual goals. Unlike the dying patients I worked with, I figured I had much more time to think about my deeper needs and wants, and so I focused on the lowest hanging fruit.

I became a victim of the money mind meld—and the only way to move forward was to learn how to see through it.

THE MONEY MIND MELD

Financial independence was originally difficult for me. I was floundering as a general internal medicine physician, trying and often failing to fight off burnout. In a completely random and fortuitous coincidence, Jim Dahle (a stranger at the time), called and asked me to review his book *The White Coat Investor* for my medical blog. When it came to money and investments, I had always considered myself savvy but by no means an expert. I jumped at the opportunity to learn something new.

His book changed my life. I quickly realized that I was already financially independent. I could leave my job and never work again! The urge to jump up and down and celebrate lasted all of a few minutes—and then I had a panic attack.

Because the fiscal transition was so abrupt, my emotional awakening was anything but smooth. Upon making the earth-shattering discovery that I was financially free, a new and unexpected dread crept into the periphery of my psyche. As the days passed, I stumbled into a full-blown depression.

At first, the reasons were quite unclear. I wallowed in anxiety and fear, but I also felt guilty for not being exhilarated.

Wasn't this exactly what I wanted?

Why am I feeling shame instead of pride?

Why doesn't this feel good?

I had fallen into a trap: the money mind meld, a trap that I would later recognize in the experiences of both Jason and Liz. Thoughts, concerns, and fears about money have an oversized role in most of our lives. Although we often think of the destructive influence such worries play in our moment-to-moment existence, there is also a protective effect.

When you concentrate on the audacious goal of financial independence or some net worth number, you push everything else aside: dreams, aspirations, and bucket list items. You become so fixated on the illusion of financial achievement that all else becomes peripheral. And why shouldn't it?

Concentrating on money is easy because it's quantifiable. It can be measured and monitored. The yardsticks are simple and the solutions straightforward: work longer, start a side hustle, invest more aggressively. Concrete questions with simple answers are more appealing than contemplating the ephemeral issues of purpose and identity. Unlike the dying, we have so much more time to consider such things. To see through the money mind meld is to realize that life is finite—to come to terms with the fact that we may die and not accomplish our true goals.

It's incredibly uncomfortable to do that.

When financial concerns are removed from the looking glass, the mirror of financial independence not only reflects but also magnifies all the inadequacies and fears that are left over: fears that are shockingly similar to the ones I encounter so often in the dying. Fears about purpose, identity, and connection. Fears that life hasn't been lived appropriately or that regrets remain.

I see the same issues arise for the newly financially independent as the ones that surface for my hospice patients when they're conducting a life review. The only difference is that for the financially independent, these issues are occurring much earlier, when the individuals are young and healthy. And that's when I realized that money and wealth are stunting our growth. They are distracting us from what is really important. The money mind meld is clouding our judgment to such an extent that it could take being diagnosed with a terminal illness to break through the haze.

We are failing to consider the key life concepts that have the most impact on day-to-day emotional well-being, self-actualization, and life satisfaction: purpose, identity, and connection. These are big concepts, so let's look at each separately.

PURPOSE

Those trapped in the money mind meld often convince themselves that wealth is the driving purpose in their lives. There is a joy in being immersed in earning, frugality, budgeting, material consumption, and tracking investments. Furthermore, there are so many quantifiable goals and landmarks to focus on along the way—it feels great to make progress.

Feeling the warmth of success, we double down on side projects and side hustles to create more cash. Optimizing income streams becomes a substitution for more elusive yet, ultimately, more satisfying pleasures. Our obsession with net worth becomes so gratifying for a moment. And then the vertigo sets in.

> ### TERMS
> **Net worth** is the total wealth of an individual, company, or household, taking account of all financial assets and liabilities.

What now? What larger purpose do we fulfill? While rest, relaxation, and travel are very appealing in the short term, one eventually has to dig into the grit of existence. Now that the money mind meld doesn't consume us, what does becoming our best self look like? Answering this question gives us our first glimpse through the money mirage. We begin to see life as it is and not some all-consuming wealth-focused vision of what it should be.

We recognize that there is still deeper, more important work to be done—work that may have nothing to do with a paycheck.

The money mind meld is a classic example of the dangers of seeing Maslow's pyramid as hierarchical. Ignoring the higher levels to solely concentrate on the lower may feel logical but often leads to depression and anxiety. We must be able to move beyond sustenance to arrive at self-actualization. This is the struggle of the newly financially independent as well as a regret of the dying. We must consider our *purpose* before we are financially independent and certainly before we become hospice patients.

Did you use that potential energy to change the world or yourself in a positive way?

Did you use your knowledge, resources, and, yes, capital to do something meaningful?

What qualifies as meaningful is completely up to you. Take Anne, a retired English professor who left her job at a prestigious city university more than a decade before I met her. Her husband died, leaving Anne alone with no children or close family. Before being diagnosed with cancer, she surrounded herself with books and magazines and discovered a completely new kind of work, unexplored during her time as a professor, as she rekindled her love of poetry. She wrote hundreds of poems while sitting in front of a roaring fire—largely ignoring the hustle and bustle of the urban sprawl occurring on the street a few stories below.

She began hospice care when her colon cancer spread to other organs. Over the months of our acquaintance, she sent several poems to literary magazines for publication. Some were accepted, others rejected. Her favorite time of day was when the mail came.

As her situation worsened, she became progressively agitated and confused. I would sit across from her quietly to give her caretaker a moment of respite. When we talked about how I, too, was interested in writing poems, she suddenly became calm. Even through the haze of delirium, she encouraged me to describe my most recent project.

Although her hold on reality was tenuous, she made me promise to bring a copy to my next visit.

Anne died quietly in her sleep. Among her unfinished papers was my poem, neatly marked with a red pen and editorial comments in the margins. Up to the moment she died, it wasn't the having or achieving that spurred her on; it was making advances toward a greater meaningful goal—the climb.

She wanted to create better poetry!

There is no right or wrong when it comes to purpose. It could be saving the whales or feeding homeless in the inner city. It could be learning martial arts or cultivating a modern art collection. When was the last time an idea kept you awake at night tossing and turning in your bed? Did you pursue it?

Your purpose doesn't have to be outwardly focused. It doesn't have to be generous. In fact, it can be downright selfish—as it was for Sam from the introduction to this book, who always had his bags packed and was ready for another adventure. Your purpose can be long-term or short-term. It can change over the years and even contradict itself. There is only one requirement.

If you can, imagine yourself lying on your deathbed bemoaning your life and saying, "I really regret that I never had the energy, courage, or time to..." Whatever comes next in that sentence is your own unique purpose. And if you are able to shake yourself awake from the money mind meld and harness that excess potential energy, you can pursue these passions long before the deterioration of old age overtakes you.

If this visualization technique fails to produce answers, there is no need to worry; it's probably time to delve into identity.

IDENTITY

Your identity is what comes directly after the words "I am." For most, that refers to our profession. *I am a doctor. I'm a lawyer.* This is often followed by important relationships: *I'm a father, husband, son.* We may even consider major accomplishments. *I am an Olympic athlete, a Nobel laureate, or the winner of such-and-such prize.*

While I don't want to make light of these kinds of answers, they feel more like factual descriptors. They describe what you are, but not necessarily *who*. Being a doctor tells me nothing about your intelligence, sense of humor, or work ethic. Knowing that you are a father may give me some insight but doesn't differentiate your values or why you make specific choices.

For years I thought being a physician was my identity. Now I realize that being a doctor is my profession—the role of a communicator is what I really identify with. How many of you are making the same mistake? Can you avoid falling into this trap?

Although my dreams were filled with activities like writing and public speaking, I crammed these passions into random nights and weekends. Becoming financially independent helped me see that my *hobbies* were more fulfilling than my so-called profession. They better define who I want to become during *the climb.*

I bet you can recognize parts of your identity that you have been denying— activities you neglect because of fear or a perceived lack of time. If not, there is no reason to panic; our identity can shift or feel less defined at times. It might take some trial and error. You may have to say yes to activities or people that you usually avoid, volunteer to do something you have never done before, or socialize with those outside your comfort zone. Ask yourself the question, What makes me feel most alive, most myself?

Identity changes over time and builds on itself. There is no perfect answer. Try repeating the phrase "I am" over and over again and see what comes next. Explore your biggest dreams and secrets without shame—see where they lead you. When you feel like you have a sense of who you are, your purpose becomes more obvious, and naturally leads to more connection.

CONNECTION

When one starts to align purpose and identity, a greater sense of connection will automatically follow. We are drawn to those with congruent values and whose passion dovetails with ours; we see them as kindred spirits. Surrounding ourselves with these types of people builds a bulwark of meaning in our lives and adds richness and texture. After all, who wants to live in a vacuum?

This becomes very obvious when caring for people who are dying. Anne, the poetess, could barely rest during her dying days. The revolving door of artists, musicians, and creatives who showed up to visit was dizzying. I was quite sure she died a wealthy woman, although you would have never known this from surveying her stark and meager apartment.

For Anne, connection was not separate from purpose and identity; it sprang from them. She built a community that would protect and nourish her—people who could share her values, losses, and victories. Even though Anne's closest relatives had died years earlier, that didn't stop her from being loved and cared for. Blood relations are sometimes less important than the chosen families we build based on a shared sense of identity and purpose.

Whom do you feel most connected to?

It is a question that I often struggled with. Although surrounded by a loving family, I often felt completely devoid of connection. I attended a large high school and a Big Ten college and felt no sense of team pride. While my classmates enjoyed football games or pep rallies, I was buried in the library studying for the next big test.

My professional life was no different. I spent no time in the doctors' lounge and hadn't befriended even a single physician colleague. At social gatherings, I steered away from conversations about work with new acquaintances. I tried my very best to hide my profession from those around me. I felt such great shame!

Only years later did I realize that the shame was unrelated to the proud profession that I had chosen. There is nothing wrong with being a physician. I was embarrassed by being identified on the outside by a title that didn't match my insides. I was a doctor by education, but my dreams were of being a communicator. The mismatch caused a lot of anxiety.

It was only after accepting the epiphany that being a physician wasn't my true identity that the pieces seemed to fall into place. I didn't like being called a doctor because I didn't identify with that professional identity. I felt no pride or status when being addressed that way. In fact, I felt disconnected—lonely.

It was only after I abandoned the physician persona and embraced the roles of communicator, speaker, and writer that I was able to build a community. Those years of feeling awkward in hospital gatherings melted away when I attended a personal finance conference or discussed blogging with a fellow writer. I finally found my people and knew that I belonged. Friendships began to blossom naturally and without friction.

I felt a much deeper sense of connection and was able to build a community of people who could nourish me as I could nourish them.

Transitioning from practicing medicine to hospice work and relating to people through speaking and writing was a less lucrative endeavor, but it built a sense of meaning and purpose totally separate from my net worth. Learning to pursue that purpose is one of the most enduring lessons I have received from the dying.

It was also one of the most difficult hurdles to overcome. There are forces that, whether intentionally or not, continually erode our ability to see past the money mirage clearly—forces that strive to maintain the status quo and keep us engaged in activities that are less than fulfilling. This is especially true when it comes to traditional work.

BEWARE: ONE-MORE-YEAR SYNDROME AND GOLDEN HANDCUFFS

There are few external motivators more insidious to realizing our unique purpose, identity, and connections than "one-more-year" syndrome and the concept of golden handcuffs. These two phenomena, one internally generated and the other put in place by our employer, are used to instill fear and incentivize against change.

The one-more-year syndrome is aptly named. Even after reaching financial stability or independence, we become a victim of the "what ifs." What if...

- The market crashes?
- Real estate evaporates?
- I can't find health care?

And then the more difficult questions arise:

- Am I anything outside of my job?
- What if this is the best it gets?
- Will my life have lost meaning?

We decide to remain in unfulfilling jobs one more year because we are afraid. *What could be the harm?* There are so many great reasons to stay: extra money, more time to plan for the future, or even corporate health care. Then a year passes, and we have the same internal debate again, and nothing has changed. Years can turn into decades. We may eventually accumulate far more material wealth than we need, but we are no closer to a greater sense of well-being or personal understanding. We are simply putting off the difficult work.

Employers have picked up on our fears and use them to their advantage. They know how expensive it is to replace key employees and provide the necessary training.

Golden handcuffs are an efficient way to coax weary employees into staying in place. Vesting bonuses, stock, end-of-year raises, and pensions that don't kick in until decades of service all await the successful employee. How can you leave so much money on the table?

> **TERMS**
>
> **Golden handcuffs** are benefits, typically deferred payments, provided by an employer to discourage an employee from accepting employment elsewhere or retiring.

Our previous definition of "enough" presupposes an external monetary goal that is our reward for fighting to the end and never giving up on our "dreams." We create our own incentives by working one more year or letting employers dangle rewards in front of us. I encourage you, though, to see *the climb*—consistent progress toward a meaningful goal—as the true objective and the more important work. And what is meaningful to you has everything to do with your unique purpose, identity, and connections, and nothing to do with your net worth.

The answer, of course, is not to abandon our careers or deny the importance that making money plays in our overall goals. But how do we better align our careers and yet stay true to our underlying purpose and identity?

One tool that continues to serve me well in this endeavor is the subject of Chapter 3: the art of subtraction.

DISCOVERING IDENTITY, PURPOSE, AND CONNECTIONS: SELF-AWARENESS QUESTIONS ON VALUES AND LIFE GOALS

1. Clear your schedule for an hour for two to three separate days over the next week. During that time, make sure all electronics are turned to silent, you are well-rested and fed, and you have found a quiet, comfortable place to concentrate.

2. Collect a pencil and two pieces of clean paper. On one, write the word "identity" at the top; on the other, write "purpose."

3. Under "identity," write the words "I am..." and use the rest of the sheet to jot down your answers. It's OK to number them if you want. You most likely will start with your job. Maybe then you will highlight your relationships ("I am a mother," "I am a daughter," and so on). Don't be afraid to get the easy stuff out of the way.

4. Now dig deeper, past work, relationships, and accomplishments. What else are you that no one knows about? Who do you strive to be? Be aspirational. What does your ideal "you" look like? When are you at your best? When do you feel most yourself?

5. You might want to put the paper down for hours or days and return to it later. Ask friends or family members. Who do they think you are? Do their lists match yours? Might they be seeing things that you are missing?

6. Now turn to the page marked "purpose," and make a list of your unique goals and dreams. If you are having difficulty defining these, take a lesson from the dying and restate the question this way: *I really regret that I never had the energy, courage, or time to...*

7. Now look over the list. Why are these dreams and goals important to you? Rank the five to ten most important items, whether they concern career, family, relationships, money, or other areas of life.

8. What proportion of your time do you dedicate to these things as opposed to more banal activities? Is your time usage aligned with what is most important to you? What could you change to correct the mismatch? Is money holding you back?

9. Lastly, look over both pages together. These will help you clarify your identity and purpose. What groups, communities, and individuals are you now drawn to? How does answering the questions in this exercise help you connect with others?

CHAPTER 3

THE "ART OF SUBTRACTION"

Do you love your job? My bet is that many would answer no. Yet one of the financial legacies my parents have given me is the model of two people who not only like their jobs, but love them. My mom is an accountant who spent most of her career helping small businesses. If not for health-related issues, I think she would do that work forever. My stepfather parlayed his C-suite success as a health care executive into a busy consulting practice that keeps him on the road even today. Early retirement was not part of their thought process, and neither was financial independence. Their W-2 wages provided enough.

In many ways, the meaning of financial independence really depends on not just your source of income, but also your feelings about your job and whether it allows you to pursue your unique purpose, identity, and connections (either on the job or outside it). In this chapter, I'll share how I've begun to see financial independence as the "art of subtraction." As I got more serious about financial independence, I began to subtract all the parts of my job that were unfulfilling or ungratifying. Then I applied the same process to life beyond work. The calculus becomes simple. Which tasks do I enjoy? Which would I rather avoid?

You might think these questions are premature or more appropriate for the wealthy and those nearing retirement. I couldn't disagree more. If I have learned anything in my line of work, it is that the future is a gift and not a guarantee. There is no time better than *now*.

THE URGENCY OF NOW

There is little that is enviable about being diagnosed with a terminal illness. There is no bright side or silver lining—with perhaps one exception: dying people understand with pure clarity the urgency of *now* and the importance of being present in the moment.

This is a small but truly consequential gift.

How many of us live with a good dose of the "once I have" syndrome? *Once I have* a significant other, I will slow down at work. *Once I have* spare cash, I will go on vacation. *Once I have* a million dollars, I will stop working nights and weekends. The list is long and is often supplemented by the closely related "once I am" syndrome. *Once I am* a doctor, I will be happy.

We spend too much time planning for an uncertain future and spurning the present, which is absolutely necessary—at times. This was stated in Chapter 2, but it bears repeating: the best time to plant a tree is twenty years ago. We have to think about tomorrow in order to plan for our future well-being. We can't enjoy our profession someday unless we receive the adequate, albeit arduous, training today. We can't bask in the glow of retirement unless we have dutifully saved and invested.

Deferred gratification, however, comes at a cost. The Stanford marshmallow experiment was a study on delayed gratification in 1972 led by psychologist Walter Mischel, a professor at Stanford University. In this study, a child was offered a choice between one reward immediately or two rewards if they waited for a number of minutes.[18] Unlike many of those young children in the study, most in the FIRE community "pass" the marshmallow test with flying colors to collect the higher bounty but forget that occasionally it is more gratifying to eat the sweet right away, and damn the consequences. Spontaneity is not always *bad*; it can also be nurturing. And just as important, our future is never guaranteed; we could die today leaving both marshmallows on the table ready for someone else to enjoy.

---

18   Walter Mischel, *The Marshmallow Test: Mastering Self-Control* (New York: Little, Brown and Company, 2014).

So how do we sort through these two extremes? How do we decide when to embrace the urgency of now and when to defer gratification? Is it possible to make the best of both?

Let's explore two concepts that magnify these extremes: YOLO and opportunity cost. Balancing these concepts will be essential to mastering the art of subtraction.

YOLO IS A NO-GO

In the past, I wrongly espoused the idea often held by the modern-day FIRE community that the YOLO mindset is the enemy of frugality. I found myself repeating the same slogan to anyone who would listen: "YOLO is a no-go."

I reasoned that you don't only live once. In their typical eighty-some years of existence, people experience many new beginnings. There are new days and new decades. New careers and new relationships. Change is so constant that we are continually beginning or ending a new stage in life.

I felt that when you make economic decisions based on the idea that once the moment has passed it will never come back again, you spend based on fear and short-lived hedonism. In actuality (especially when young), every new stage in life will feel like a fresh start. Although wisdom accrues, new beginnings abound.

I used to believe that when young people spend as if they only live once, they eventually face a multitude of new life stages poor and unprepared to fully enjoy what life has to offer. Think of all the joys a young parent or a newly retired person can experience when they have enough economic fuel to propel their journey.

And let's not forget that money compounds. If you carry YOLO to the extreme, you may accrue little in your bank account; empty coffers don't multiply! If you front-load the sacrifice at the beginning of your career, on the other hand, wealth accumulates at a much faster rate. By the time you reach middle age you will have enough to YOLO more aggressively than you ever imagined.

YOLO, to me, was a battle cry that focused on fear: since you only live once, you better grab those opportunities before they disappear forever.

And then I started caring for the dying who would give any amount of money for a little bit of time or a few more memorable experiences.

How could my stance on YOLO not change?

Since then, I have come to believe the majority of our spending should be on either joy or necessity—not on fear. To become a master of the art of subtraction (as we will soon see) is to be choosy about what we can and can't live without. We can always be open to a new adventure as well as allow some of our money to compound in investments. Your dollars should be used to embrace the good things, not chase the ephemeral, nor be locked away forever in some bank account.

Of course, there is such a thing as opportunity cost, but it is, for the most part, a fallacy.

THE OPPORTUNITY COST FALLACY

We make decisions based on opportunity cost all the time, although we are rarely conscious of it. It is the cost of choosing one alternative over another and, in the process, missing the benefit offered by not having made that choice. Have you ever been lurking in a financial forum when a member is castigated for relishing an expensive purchase? The naysayers argue that the same money invested wisely could compound to much higher sums.

This argument makes perfect sense if money is the most important predefined end point—if you have succumbed to the money mind meld. I call this mistake the opportunity cost fallacy: confusing the value of money (compounded or not) more than what you have traded it for. Let's dive a little deeper.

A repeated belief that exacerbates the opportunity cost fallacy is that we lose the opportunity to let our money grow and compound. While this belief is true, it is shortsighted to conclude that the trade-off is always worthwhile. For instance, certain experiences occur only once in a life-time and are well worth spending on.

Ernesto, a middle-aged man dying rapidly of leukemia, regaled the hospice team with stories of his climbing expedition to Mount Everest: "I didn't eat out or travel for a whole year before!"

There were sacrifices that impacted both his lifestyle and his bank account. Yet, lying in bed waiting to die, neither the lost luxury nor the lost revenue weighed on his mind; what he remembered was the utter joy of feeling his muscles contract as he heaved his body toward the summit. It was money well spent.

Imagine you are financially stable and have enough money. Once your investments and side hustles cover your yearly expenses, everything left over is extra. Might there come a time when spending a few thousand dollars (or a few hundred thousand if you're lucky) just doesn't move the needle? On the other hand, that beautiful painting that hangs in your room, or that speedy car in your driveway, may actually bring real joy. It may give you pleasure for decades.

While it is financially responsible to plan for the future and save for a long and healthy retirement, it shouldn't be accomplished at the expense of the urgency of now. We must remember that opportunity costs are about so much more than money; experience, relationships, and knowl-edge also compound. As human beings, we need to eat, to breathe, and to have shelter. Sometimes we also need to covet, to have adventure, and to experience the best money can buy. There is no shame in trading wealth for enjoyment and memories. Money was meant to be used.

You can have both an emergency fund and a YOLO fund. In fact, this might be the easiest way to reconcile the issue. Spending money, taking time off of work, and even frivolity can be budgeted into your lifestyle. That way, when the opportunity arises, you can take advantage of the joy of spontaneity and not have it derail all your plans. You can pay homage to the urgency of now by always having a bag packed as well as a bank account in good standing and a career worth fighting for.

If you are having trouble coming to terms with the opportunity cost fallacy, maybe it's time to turn to the chronically ill and dying. What's their perspective?

REGRETS OF THE DYING

Bronnie Ware, Australian author, songwriter, and palliative care nurse, wrote the transformational book *The Top Five Regrets of the Dying* in 2012.[19] While administering hospice and palliative care to those who were in their last weeks of life, she asked about regrets: What would the dying do differently if they had more time? The most common answers became one of the world's most famous top five lists, "the top five regrets of the dying":

1. I wish I'd had the courage to live a life true to myself, not the life others expected of me.

2. I wish I hadn't worked so hard.

3. I wish I'd had the courage to express my feelings.

4. I wish I had stayed in touch with my friends.

5. I wish that I had let myself be happier.

You can hear echoes of the urgency of now, YOLO, and the opportunity cost fallacy in almost every regret listed above. For instance, "I wish I'd had the courage to live a life true to myself" smacks of unfulfilled and delayed dreams. Maybe instead of delaying our bucket list items, we should pursue them before it's too late, before surpassing those horrible *once I have* or *once I am* requirements. There is no time like the present. *Carpe diem!*

"I wish I hadn't worked so hard" speaks to the dangers of delayed gratification. Although we have to plan for the future, delayed gratification can most certainly go too far. As noted in Chapter 1, we are working more hours than ever and more nights and weekends, and we are taking less vacation. We are becoming blinded by the money mind meld and seeing

---

19 Bronnie Ware, *The Top Five Regrets of the Dying: A Life Transformed by the Dearly Departing* (Carlsbad, CA: Hay House, 2012).

wealth as an objective as opposed to the tool it was meant to be. We are not using our precious potential energy to accomplish what really has meaning for us.

The third and fourth regrets may not directly touch on monetary issues, but the lessons are no less salient to our conversation. We must have the courage to do difficult things, forgo the easier pathway, and do today what we could defer until tomorrow.

I'll refer back to our discussion of whether money can buy happiness when discussing the fifth regret: *I wish that I had let myself be happier.* The two types of happiness that researchers evaluate are emotional well-being and life evaluation. A plethora of studies show wealth has limited effects on both once we account for basic needs and safety.

So how do we take these regrets of the dying and use them to impact or own lives now? How do we incorporate the urgency of now, partake appropriately of YOLO, and not become a victim of the opportunity cost fallacy? Maybe we should ask Sam, who always had his bags packed and journeyed to many exotic locales before his unfortunate death. He realized that you can't take your money with you, and so he lived his last days like he was dying—because he was. Wouldn't it be wonderful if those of us in the midst of life could integrate such thinking before our circumstances became so dire?

I COULD'VE USED A LITTLE YOLO

I could have used a little more of the YOLO attitude during those difficult years when I was building a career, amassing wealth, and nurturing my family. I was the typical victim of the "once I have/once I am" syndrome. I deferred once-in-a-lifetime trips with family and friends to Australia when I was in college, to Moscow in medical school, and to Italy with my kids when I was a practicing physician. I deferred gratification, ignoring the urgency of now because I was always too busy. I didn't understand that I was barreling toward some amorphous monetary goal—some ill-defined version of "enough" that I was unlikely to ever find fulfilling. I was on course to become the absolutely richest guy in the cemetery.

My bags weren't packed. I was in no position to jump headfirst into the quirky life opportunities that fortuitously came my way. I never gave myself a chance to really live—to be spontaneous, to let go of the future, and spend a little cash for immediate gratification. My father's death at the tender age of forty should have been a cold splash of water in my face—but it wasn't.

Perhaps I was afraid of having the same fate as my father. My fear of dying was hampering me. It was much easier to focus on wealth building than doing the harder work of exploring my own purpose, identity, and connections. I struggled to face mortality head on and realize that, like my father, I might not be here next week, month, or year. If I put on blinders and only concentrated on wealth, then everything would be OK. I gritted my teeth and muddled through a profession that was no longer fulfilling because it allayed deeper worries that I wasn't ready or able to face.

Why didn't I have the courage to live a life that was true to myself? Why have I worked so hard? Why don't I have the courage to express my feelings? Why don't I stay in touch with my friends? Why don't I allow myself to be happy?

I was destined to fall into the trap of the money mind meld and be none the wiser—until my trajectory was altered significantly on a quiet winter day in 2014.

While seeing patients in the office, I received that call from Jim Dahle. Reading his book would introduce me to the financial independence movement and help me realize that I had enough money to do whatever I wanted with my precious time and career.

Freedom from the economic bonds of my profession helped me develop a superpower that I now recognize as essential to navigating the divide between money and purpose regardless of one's current wealth: the art of subtraction. I could simply get rid of all those aspects of my professional career that no longer nurtured me. All I had to ask was one simple question:

Does this activity give me a deeper sense of purpose, identity, or connections?

I became a master of the art of subtraction. I immediately stopped working on nights and weekends—I could off-load those hours on someone else.

Then I removed myself from the call schedule. Who wants to be woken up in the middle of the night on a regular basis?

Each time I stepped away from an unenjoyable task, I created a work environment that better matched my internal desires. By the time I was finished, hospice was the only professional activity left. It was the part of the job I would do even if I wasn't getting paid.

Isn't that the best litmus test?

What would you keep if money was not an issue?

I am not unaware of the fact that when I discovered the art of subtraction, I was in a very privileged position financially. My net worth as a doctor had grown over the years and afforded me quite a bit of flexibility. You might not feel like you are beginning from a place of such strength. Maybe you have student loan debt or are struggling at a minimum-wage job. This shouldn't, however, stop you from evaluating the trade-offs in your life that affect both your finances and your happiness. You might find yourself in dire circumstances, as my wife's family did when she was a child. What will you do then?

The year 1979 was a devastating one for my in-laws. The rise of the Ayatollah Khomeini and the removal of the shah of Iran was the beginning of a family crisis that would have permanent and long-ranging consequences. My father-in-law was promptly arrested and thrown in jail for being the chief financial officer of a multinational company that had ties to the previous government. Upon his release, a stark choice became hauntingly clear. Stay in Iran surrounded by prestige, wealth, and everything the family had ever known, or leave to secure their personal safety and freedom in the United States.

The family left one day, under a shroud of secrecy, leaving property, bank accounts, and lucrative jobs behind to come to Chicago, Illinois, with little more than the clothes on their backs, to live a life of poverty. My father-in-law quit a high-paying position as a chief financial officer to perform whatever bookkeeping jobs were available to someone without a formal college education. My mother-in-law, the proud matron of a wealthy Iranian family, took a job as a nanny for a neighbor's young twins.

By necessity, they became experts of the art of subtraction. They simply couldn't afford whatever was unnecessary. Instead of living in a spacious four-bedroom house, all five of them packed into a two-bedroom apartment. The latest Iranian fashions were discarded for thrift store fare. They never even considered eating out at a restaurant for their first decade in the United States.

As friends and family in better circumstances with more sustainable careers arrived in the US, my wife's family found themselves feeling left behind. They no longer had the outward material signs of wealth and success that had been their hallmark before becoming immigrants. While their counterparts were buying Mercedes and BMWs, my father-in-law was stuck with a decades-old used Toyota. The pressure was immense to beg, borrow, or steal to keep up with the Iranian Joneses.

But my in-laws didn't give in to the pressure. They carefully saved and were able to eventually move out of the apartment into a modest three-bedroom home. After my father-in-law was held up at gunpoint while working in a shoe store, he was able to take their meager savings and use it as a down payment to buy a building. Like the decision to leave Iran, his careful planning allowed him to use the art of subtraction to rid himself of what had become a tiresome and dangerous job. This building would sustain his family over the next few decades. But like all of the other decisions he courageously made, it came at a cost; he often had to race over himself in the middle of the night to manage emergency repairs because he couldn't afford a handyman.

Now approaching ninety years old, my father-in-law has spent much time reviewing his life, as so many of my hospice patients do. Although he will always lament having had to leave Iran, he would never say that doing so wasn't worth it. Leaving wealth and prestige behind, forgoing the luxuries that were really of lesser value, will always be secondary. He can look at his thriving children and grandchildren and know that freedom, opportunity, and safety were worth the difficult decisions.

"Driving an expensive car was never really that great anyway!"

What could you do even in the most dire of circumstances to become a master of the art of subtraction? Could you switch jobs, change locations, or live on less? What levers do you have available to pull?

FINANCIAL INDEPENDENCE IS A LEVER

The art of subtraction helped me realize that financial independence is about so much more than just money. How do you feel about your job? Is it sustaining you? Is it leading to a greater sense of meaning and purpose? If so, then maybe financial freedom is possible even for those whose coffers are less than full. If not, then it is best to see financial independence in the more traditional role as a lever.

Let's return to the example of my parents. After paying for all their children's college educations, my parents had more than enough money to retire from their jobs as a certified public accountant (CPA) and a health care consultant. Yet both of them felt that they were just digging into their careers. They had spent a lifetime of accumulating, creating an extremely powerful lever—a lever that they decided not to pull. Neither of them was ready to walk away from their careers just yet.

But that doesn't mean that they didn't have options. The art of subtraction was ever present in their decision-making. As their careers grew, they were able to hone their daily activities to enhance what they enjoyed and subtract out the rest. Clients were dropped. Accounts were closed.

In my own life, as I began to become more and more financially stable, I employed the same art of subtraction on a regular basis. I slowly replaced all the responsibilities that were unfulfilling or ungratifying. Then I looked at those things that I didn't enjoy doing at home.

For instance, I have no fondness for doing lawn work. The calculus then becomes quite simple. What do I enjoy (or dislike) more: doing some of the more mundane activities at work or coming home to a messy yard? For me, the answer was a no-brainer.

There were plenty of tasks that I was needed for on the job that were less annoying than trimming the bushes. I might not be paid as much as previously, but I would make enough to hire a lawn care service as well as chip in for some other domestic activities that I don't enjoy.

I know—right about now you're thinking: *Well, that may be great for you, but what if I can't stand my job?*

I don't want to suggest that you should love your work. Many don't. In fact, some studies show that work satisfaction in America has been in steady decline since the 1980s and into the aughts. These numbers have somewhat increased since 2010.[20] But the recent record migration away from employment, dubbed the Great Resignation, points to widespread discontent. Sometimes you do have to throw the baby out with the bathwater. Traditional early retirement may be your best choice. There is no shame here. This is where diligent saving and investing becomes exceedingly important. The only way to completely leave the workforce is to have been building a significant nest egg over the years.

But most of us don't hate work.

The more likely scenario is that you don't have enough to retire yet and feel rather underwhelmed by work—you don't love or hate it. Welcome to the party; you are like the vast majority of Americans. This is why it is critical to start building a bridge to traditional financial independence. You might not want to radically change your life, but you also feel the tug of the urgency of now. This is the perfect time to consider alternatives like Slow FI and Coast FI—plans that allow for a retirement glide path. You can take your sweet time planning the ideal asset allocation, stuffing those IRAs (individual retirement accounts) or 529s, or waiting for a child to mature.

Meanwhile, you can use the art of subtraction to improve your quality of life immediately. Maybe working part-time or forgoing the difficult client will cost you in terms of income and delay retirement to some later

---

20   G. Levanon, A. L. Abel, A. Li, and C. Rong, "Job Satisfaction 2021," The Conference Board, https://www.conference-board.org/pdfdownload.cfm?master ProductID=27278.

date. But isn't that worth a little relief immediately? How can you create options even if your finances are not yet completely in order?

When we reimagine our relationship with our jobs, we leave behind the sense of victimhood and start to exert control over how we spend our time. The art of subtraction gives us power and allows us to be in control of the chess pieces.

DECIDING WHAT TO SUBTRACT

The art of subtraction should be wielded like a scalpel and not a sword. Life design by nature is a delicate process. It is easy to make a decision you will eventually regret at the end of a hard day before the consequences are fully thought out. I experienced this many times in medicine. Many days, I walked out of the hospital or office swearing that I would never return again. Thankfully, after quiet reflection, I realized I was reacting to momentary emotions. Before departing from any activity, it makes sense to think carefully about what is being left behind. I usually ask myself a few basic questions.

Does this activity add to my underlying sense of purpose, identity, and connection? When I found financial independence, my first reaction was to walk away from medicine completely. I was burned out and beaten down. And these are not feelings exclusive to the medical field. Anyone in any job position can feel these exact emotions. You've probably felt them yourself. Can you blame me for wanting to leave?

Upon deeper reflection, I realized that the core of being a physician—helping and teaching—was still very much a part of my identity. It was the late nights, paperwork hassles, and lack of time with patients that no longer fit. I also came to the conclusion that medicine was taking on an oversized portion of my identity. I didn't want to abandon medicine completely; I just wanted to create more room for creativity and communication.

What are the trade-offs? Life was not meant to be stress-free. Sometimes, in order to pursue things we really want, we have to suffer for a time. We shouldn't immediately subtract an activity just because we don't like it.

While I have always loved to write and have dreamed of being an author, I absolutely despise the process of editing and rewriting. It is a trade-off, however, that I am willing to make to ultimately reach my goals.

As vivid as Ernesto's memories were of climbing to the base camp of Mount Everest, there were other memories he would rather forget. There was little joy in those five a.m. workouts that he endured for years before he was physically ready to make the climb. He clearly understood the trade-offs and was willing to do unenjoyable things in order to ultimately accomplish something that was very meaningful for him.

Am I benefiting my community—and the world? Joe was a veteran of many not-for-profit boards over the years. He had presided over a number of successful companies and charities. Although his prostate cancer had spread throughout his bones, he had to cancel his meeting with the hospice nurse in order to join a Zoom call for an urgent board meeting for one of his charities. I offhandedly commented about how he must love his work.

He responded, "Those calls—they bore the heck out of me!"

Joe knew, however, that his expertise was making a difference in other people's lives. He might not always enjoy the moment-to-moment chores involved, but philanthropy and service were very much tied to his sense of identity and purpose.

Like Ernesto and Joe, we must carefully decide what to subtract from our lives and why. We must remember that although at moments *the climb* can be arduous, that shouldn't necessarily cause us to let go of important goals and dreams. We shouldn't give up that easily.

Not only should we evaluate our activities, but we should also look at our spending with a similar lens. *Am I spending to "keep up with the Joneses"?* How much of the monthly budget is allocated to material objects or activities that in the end add little value to our lives? They may create the outward appearance of *success* or *happiness*, but in reality, such objects and activities place us squarely on an unrelenting treadmill. We run faster and faster but come no closer to self-actualization. Subtracting unnecessary budget items and unused luxuries may make working part-time a real possibility. How much more nourishing work could we accomplish when freed from the nine-to-five? How many hours could be spent with family and friends?

Although you may not feel particularly good at tracking your budget, that should not stop you from using the art of subtraction when it comes to spending. In fact, my family suffers from this very issue.

Instead, we utilize a concept called the nonbudget.

SUBTRACTION AND THE NONBUDGET

Almost everywhere we look, there are budgeting tips and tricks to make the most of our dollar. Because many of us are limited in how much we can make each year, to accelerate our path to financial independence we have to be very mindful of how we spend money. There are a few ways to accomplish this very important task. Some of us are trackers by nature and enjoy using apps and spreadsheets. We budget traditionally by signing into Personal Capital or Mint every month or by using good old paper and pencil and categorizing expenditures line by line. We know exactly where each penny goes and do our best to minimize waste. While this may work for some, I am a bigger fan of what I like to call the nonbudget. I freely admit that we are a disorganized, nonbudget bunch in my household. Our organizational style seems to have a touch of attention deficit disorder and doesn't always conform perfectly to the accountant's ledger book. Instead, we have to find ways to budget without using the laser-like precision that many savers employ.

Our simple way around this conundrum is to build frugality into our daily habits. Over the years we've formed several savings habits that require almost no thought or energy. In fact, in many ways I would call this lazy or low-energy budgeting.

How can you nonbudget like us without straining to make it work? Here are a few simple ideas:

1. We never carry cash, and almost never use our ATM cards. If you happen to be with me at a conference or meeting, don't expect that I'll have an extra quarter for the vending machine. My wallet is totally empty. It's fairly laughable for a family with a good income and two professionals. But if you don't have the cash immediately available, you are unlikely to spend on cash-only items. This means that we have cut down on vending machine, junk food, and other unplanned purchases that are usually more frivolous than necessary. As a side note, this habit also helps us stay healthy because we are bypassing fatty and sugary processed foods and drinks.

2. We are a two-income family, but we live like a one-income family. From the moment that we both started earning wages, one paycheck automatically gets deposited directly to a savings or brokerage account. There is no fuss or drama over spending. We either have enough in our checking account or not. We automate our savings, and they are not part of our budget. That money is gone. *C'est la vie.*

3. We let the kids budget themselves. My wife and I have made the kids responsible for their own buying habits. They get a certain amount of allowance each year. If they run out too fast, they suffer the consequences. There are no surprises in this column of the ledger.

4. We rarely buy big-ticket items in stores, we never buy big-ticket items on a whim, and we bargain hunt. Our purchases are well researched and often there is a cooling-off period between the excitement of the decision to buy and the actual date of consumption.

Not being organized and mathematical does not prohibit you from being frugal and wise with your spending. For our family, the nonbudget seems to check all of our subtraction boxes. It is easy, effective, and causes minimal disruption in our daily lives.

Our nonbudget is a perfect example of how to incorporate subtraction smoothly into your busy life. There comes a time, however, when the art of subtraction can no longer be subtle—when it should become less of an art and more of a necessity.

NEVER DESPISE WORK

As with just about everything, there is nuance in these decisions. The idea is not to dispense of the shades of gray, but rather to study them. We need to be more thoughtful not only about what we spend our money on, but also about what we refuse to spend money on.

The art of subtraction is a good starting place, but it can only take us so far. My work with the dying has taught me that life is too precious to spend our time doing a job we despise. Yes, we might need to front-load our work if we want to retire sooner—but that's not the same thing as signing up for a job that makes us absolutely miserable.

If you are in a job that you hate right now, it is time to consider immediate changes. It might be as simple as looking to continue doing the same work but for a different employer. If the work itself is the problem, are there skills, passions, or resources available that will enable you to pivot?

After two decades of teaching, Cyrus, a patient I cared for who had end-stage lung damage due to smoking, remembers being ready to call it quits as a math instructor. He didn't have the resources to retire and was petrified at the prospect of leaving his hefty teaching pension behind. Becoming the high school's college counselor and coaching the varsity soccer team fortuitously spared him the difficult decision to leave the district. Even years after retirement, he continued to help on the sidelines during games until his breathing problems became too severe. When asked on his deathbed, Cyrus admitted that he ended up loving his job.

Like Cyrus, there may be solutions to your work situation that both provide income and increase your quality of life. That's why, in Part Two, we're going to explore our personal work and lifestyles so that you can decide which trade-offs you're willing to make and which ones are deal-breakers. There are many paths to financial independence; the key is finding the one that's right for you.

PRACTICING THE ART OF SUBTRACTION: THE REVERSE LOTTERY TEST

1. Clear your schedule for an hour for two to three separate days over the next week. During that time, make sure all electronics are turned to silent, you are well-rested and fed, and you have found a quiet, comfortable place to concentrate.

2. Close your eyes and imagine that you flipped on the television and learned that your megabillions lottery ticket just hit the mark. Time to go out to the pub and celebrate! Take a moment to bask in the relief and joy you feel in never having to worry about money again—you're home free.

3. Think about all those things your newfound wealth is going to allow you to buy: a new home, car, maybe the latest iPhone. What will it feel like?

4. Now open your eyes and either turn on your phone's scheduling app or, if you are old-fashioned, thumb through the next week in your daily planner. What types of activities are filling your days?

5. How many of these activities are contributing to your overall sense of purpose, identity, and connections? How many do you dread? How many would you pay someone else to perform if money were not an option?

6. Think carefully. Mentally subtract all those activities that don't bring you joy and would now be unnecessary. Was money the deciding factor? If not, what has stopped you from ditching these activities sooner? Fear? Guilt?

7. You have now performed the reverse lottery test on your schedule and used the art of subtraction to better align your schedule with your deeper sense of meaning and purpose. What did you learn?

8. Finally, consider how much you would need to save in order to make these changes even without winning the lottery. Are there ways to accomplish this goal before you reach financial independence?

Could you use tools like Slow FI or Coast FI to get there faster? Would a job change or a move to another geographic location better help you reach your goals?

9. Don't stress if the answers aren't clear at this point. These are not questions that have an expiration date. Try to meditate on them from time to time. Look at your schedule every week and ask, What could be subtracted today and why?

PART TWO

MANY PATHS
TO FINANCIAL
INDEPENDENCE

CHAPTER 4

THE PARABLE OF THE THREE BROTHERS

In the preceding chapter, we looked at the art of subtraction. But how do we decide what to subtract if we misjudge what actually motivates us and are deluded about what we truly want? How do we design the ideal life if we have a distorted definition of happiness? How do we know how to recognize "enough"?

When we are unclear about our internal motivation, our end goal becomes less gratifying. I first experienced this phenomenon in my weight-loss journey. A few years back, I discovered an app called My Fitness Pal, which allowed me to track my eating habits, including daily calorie intake, macronutrient makeup, and even calories burned during exercise. When I became aware of exactly what I was eating, the pounds quickly disappeared. Every day, I would marvel at the way my body was transforming in the mirror—until I didn't.

At some point my mind became so accustomed to my transformed body that it no longer felt *new*. It felt, well, regular. In fact, I began to seize on tiny imperfections I'd never noticed before. Looking in the mirror became upsetting—I felt lost and confused. My anxiety further multiplied when I realized these feelings were pervasive in other parts of my life.

It felt shockingly like the money mind meld. Even though your net worth might be climbing, you don't feel any happier. No real transformation has occurred apart from numbers on a balance sheet.

How do you measure improvement when you haven't clearly defined your goals? How do you bask in success when you don't understand your true motivation?

When we evaluate our achievements in the rearview mirror, most of us realize that the joy was in surmounting obstacles. Overcoming desperation, setting a plan, and making progress are what happiness actually looks like. What truly differentiates us as individuals is the road we decide to take and why. How can we use that knowledge to lead to a deeper understanding of not only our finances but other aspects of our lives?

INTERNAL VERSUS EXTERNAL MOTIVATION

There once was a curmudgeonly old man who lived in a small house at the end of the street. His true joy was the unassuming plot of grass leading to his humble abode. The neighborhood kids also adored this same patch of lawn, particularly to extend their football games from the adjacent lot. Trample, trample, trample: they gleefully tore up the poor man's little piece of heaven.

Try as he might, he couldn't stop or change the children's behavior. He screamed. He threatened. His impassioned pleas fell on unsympathetic ears—until the day he smartened up. Being all too aware of the relationship between internal and external motivation that even children fall prey to, he came up with a plan.

He offered each child ten dollars to play on his lawn daily. He persuaded them that it was beneficial for the soil.

The children were overjoyed—not only were they disburdened of his daily verbal lashing, they also received monetary encouragement to do exactly what they wanted.

And so they played, and their hearts were content—for a while. Until the wily old man began to turn the screws.

The second week, his strategy was different. Although he was still happy to have them play on his lawn, the old man scolded the children for a suboptimal performance and offered five dollars instead. Maybe if they improved, he would reconsider next payday.

Miffed, the kids hemmed and hawed but eventually took the five dollars. And so they played and their hearts were content—if not but a little less. Their pockets were not quite as full.

Finally, the homeowner threw down the gauntlet. He was downright disgruntled with their state of play. For all he cared, the kids could use his lawn as much as they wanted. But there would be no more cash. They would have to do it for free.

The children considered the situation briefly. As their venom rose, they shrugged their shoulders and stomped off the lawn, and vowed, until the day they died, that they would never, ever play on the old man's lawn again.

This is classic behavioral theory.

Placing external rewards on tasks we are internally motivated to accomplish often has catastrophic consequences. Such rewards can take the form of money, prestige, or even feelings of self-worth based on some number on the scale.

No wonder my physical appearance left me feeling unsatisfied during my weight-loss journey. As long as I was using an external metric to gauge progress, I had lost touch with my true motivation, which was internal: to be healthy and feel better. Likewise, when it came to money, the reward of a large net worth failed to capture my true wish of exerting more control over my time.

Rewards don't quench our internal motivations. This is an especially important point to remember when dealing with wealth accumulation. Only when we understand what drives us can we then go about building a fulfilling life—creating the right balance between delayed gratification and the urgency of now.

But how do we recognize what drives us?

The answer—whether we are figuring out how to manage our finances or how to be more physically fit—is to discover what we are most intrinsically motivated to do. When given the options, which is the right path?

I believe a parable, the story of the three brothers, can help point us in the right direction.

THE THREE BROTHERS

There once were three very different brothers who set off on the journey of a lifetime by embarking on three separate roads. Because each brother was unique, these roads diverged quickly.

The eldest brother was considered the most efficient, so it was unsurprising that he chose a path that was straight and clear of time-wasting roadblocks. The middle brother was a strong walker but easily distracted; there were many detours along the way. He had trouble concentrating on the task at hand. And, finally, the youngest was known as something of a noncon-formist. He neither moved forward too quickly nor got distracted too easily. He was just slow—deliberate.

The Eldest Brother

The eldest of the three brothers had a concrete goal in mind, for he had no fondness for the road; he never enjoyed hiking. He saw the end as a destination, a culmination of his struggles. His thirst for finishing was so great that he often skipped meals and sleep to plod farther along.

He suffered greatly but made significant progress in a short time. His physical fatigue and emotional weakness were buoyed by dreams of all the things he could do once he reached his desti-nation. If only he could get there faster, he would be free—free to travel to foreign lands, or, even better, climb the tallest moun-tains.

These dreams were the steam in his engine, the gas in his car.

When he finally came to the end of his journey, he did indeed enjoy a long period of freedom. Although the road had battered him both mentally and physically, it was a sacrifice he had been more than willing to make.

The Middle Brother

The middle of the three brothers also wasn't overly fond of his particular road. But he lacked the strength and determination of the eldest brother. He thus decided to split his journey into more manageable increments. When he found his energy running low, he would follow a flight of fancy into the fields or up a mountain.

Although these trips off the prescribed path lengthened the middle brother's journey and cost him in terms of time, he found his joy refreshed and his stamina rebuilt with each extracurricular foray.

It was many years after the elder brother that the middle brother reached the end of his road. He had less time to enjoy his new freedom but a good deal more energy.

The Youngest Brother

The youngest brother was much slower and more deliberate than his elders. In fact, he loved to hike. So instead of looking at the road as a destination, he saw the path as a joyful journey. He took time to notice the trees and rivers, the seasons changing, the sun on his face. He felt no need to hurry.

When he finally reached his destination, he did something neither of his brothers could understand. He turned around and started to walk back the way he came.

* * *

The three brothers represent many things. They can help us understand our relationship with employment—how we see our jobs and what role they play in our lives. Or they could be a metaphor for how we approach not only work but relationships, achievements, and fulfillment in general. After all, as the saying goes, how you do anything is how you do everything.

Were they to undergo the life review practice I shared in Chapter 1, the three brothers would report satisfaction in very different ways. The eldest would point to various achievements and feel proud at how quickly he reached the destination but perhaps wonder whether he could have enjoyed the road a bit more. The middle would focus neither on the road itself nor on the destination but would savor the unexpected side forays, trips, and various adventures off the beaten path. He would often question whether he could have taken more chances with his money, turned it into more experiences and opportunities to pack his bags.

And the youngest would regale us with stories of the road and all its glory. He would have so enjoyed the journey that he could be oblivious to the fact that there is also joy in measuring and assessing a final outcome. The third brother would be happy to die on the road, just as Bobbie, whom we met in the introduction, was happy to die in the office of his store with the next deal just a signature away.

Does any of this sound like you?

Let's delve more deeply into the characteristics of each brother, and you can consider which of their paths resonate most.

CHOICE 1: THE TRADITIONAL PATH—FRONT-LOAD THE SACRIFICE

"He wouldn't let me put the thermostat above 70 degrees!"

Herb's wife chuckled as she sat across from his now-empty bed. He was a stickler about such things after leaving dentistry in his late forties. They had squirreled away a small nest egg, which would grow in the stock market and fund almost five decades of retirement. Of course, there were some sacrifices. They moved from the expensive suburbs of New Jersey to Santa Fe, New Mexico, in the early 1960s.

> **TERMS**
>
> **Geographic arbitrage** is the process of moving from a high-cost-of-living area to a low-cost-of-living area. Spending less makes your money go farther and supercharges the path to financial independence.

Herb and his wife utilized frugality, investing, and geographic arbitrage—dubbed "geoarbitrage" by the FIRE community—to free themselves from an unsatisfying career choice. While they made decisions carefully, the trade-offs (such as the low thermostat setting) were well worth the almost fifty years spent traveling the world, volunteering, and spending time with friends and family.

This is the road of the eldest brother.

The eldest brother's journey represents what I often call the "American dream script"—the idea that hard work and sacrifice make up the quickest path to happiness and wealth. Perhaps because this idea is so deeply ingrained in our culture, this approach was embraced by many of the original FIRE practitioners, such as Mr. Money Mustache and J. D. Roth, the renowned author of the blog *Get Rich Slowly*. They parlayed stable salaries and wise money management into financial stability and early retirement.

This path is often chosen by those of us who suspect that we'll never love our jobs. Whether it be early retirement or a particular net worth, we have a goal in mind, and we're willing to put in the extra hours, lose sleep, or work weekends to get there. The promise is a future where we don't need to earn any extra income over and above the return on our investments.

Following the road of the eldest brother requires rapidly accumulating enough assets to build a secure nest egg. Exponential net worth growth is garnered by high savings rates, frugality, and stock investing. The power of compounding is a key ingredient in shortening the length of time until retirement. Money saved in the first decade of employment is squirreled away into tax-deferred accounts, and employer matches are welcomed.

Eldest brothers are often professionals who start with typical wage earning through third-party employment. Although the same results can be achieved with real-estate investing or entrepreneurship, we often see this tactic with white-collar workers such as doctors, lawyers, engineers, and computer consultants.

It would be a mistake, however, to say that an ultrahigh income is necessary. There are many teachers, tradespeople, and lower-wage earners who have also used this technique. They are experts at minding the gap—working both the income and savings sides of the equation. Even on a meager paycheck, they expertly use frugality and other life hacks to reach their net worth goals.

FRONT-LOAD THE SACRIFICE

Front-loading the sacrifice is the main tool utilized by eldest brothers. It bluntly requires, as the name suggests, sacrifice. It is the opposite of YOLO. One must delay the urgency of now, in the short term, to reap the benefits in the future. After all, getting to financial independence requires hard work, planning, and often, missed opportunities. While, ideally, we both climb the mountain and enjoy the beauty of the local terrain at the same time, this path requires a concrete end in mind that can be tracked with laser-like focus. As we discussed earlier, although this process alone will not ultimately lead to greater emotional well-being—we still have to better understand our own unique meaning and purpose—building a solid economic foundation is a good start.

TERMS

Front-loading is distributing or allocating costs, effort, and so on unevenly, with the greater proportion at the beginning of the enterprise or process.

The path of the eldest brother is most akin to flying a jumbo jet across the Atlantic. Every pilot knows that the greatest expenditure of energy occurs during takeoff. Once the plane reaches cruising altitude, however, fuel needs decrease drastically.

Your financial timeline is no different. The fuel burned early in the journey will often propel you even faster for the rest of the trip. This is particularly important in your early twenties.

Don't believe me?

As a resident physician, I moonlighted at my local hospital and saved $10,000 for a down payment on our first house. We sold that house a few years later for a profit and invested $50,000 dollars into index funds. After twenty years, that smaller sum that started as extra cash from nights and weekends has multiplied into enough to comfortably pay for both my kids' college educations. And there will be plenty left over! It's not just compounding gains, but also compounding losses; credit costs money. If you have residual educational or car loans, you're sapping your jet fuel every month in the form of interest. That interest will erode your wealth and hamper your path to financial freedom. Some of you left undergraduate education with a mountain of debt. Whether you demolish that mountain or let it grow even higher will have profound consequences on your financial well-being.

My wife had $15,000 of educational debt when she finished college. We both put in extra hours at work in those early years to pay it off fairly quickly. We sacrificed our time and energy while we were young. By becoming debt-free, we were able to maximize retirement savings and start a taxable brokerage account at the beginning of our careers.

I can imagine right about now you are thinking, *What's the rush? Why not enjoy life a little while I'm still young?*

The truth, unfortunately, is that the clock is ticking. There are several advantages to starting on the path of the eldest brother right out of high school or college. You don't have as many overarching responsibilities weighing you down, such as children or a costly mortgage. You are free to aggressively pursue a career, business opportunity, or side hustle. As you get older, have children, and settle into suburbia, your time becomes parsed between competing demands screaming for your attention—you won't have as much time!

Young people also have an abundance of energy. As a new physician, I could work thirty-six hours straight without requiring a minute of sleep. Now, it takes weeks to recover from such activities.

Front-loading the sacrifice at the beginning of your career can create endless possibilities. It will propel you through the stratosphere and prepare the way for coasting at a comfortable altitude. Once you've cleared takeoff, it will be time to focus on your proposed destination.

Which direction are you traveling? How will you know when you have arrived? We will cover these topics more in upcoming chapters.

THE RISKS OF THE ELDEST

By far, the greatest risk to eldest brothers is their own mortality. Front-loading is a great technique for those who expect to live decades into the future. But if we become overly focused on our monetary goals, we may spend far too much precious time in the process of building wealth that will never serve us. Eldest brothers must always be aware of the gruesome possibility that life may be short; death could come unexpectedly at any time. While delaying gratification is important, eldest brothers also must be careful to allocate some time, energy, and even money to attaining important life goals now. When Ernesto took six months off of work to pursue his climbing expedition on Mount Everest, he had no idea that a terminal illness would befall him less than a decade later.

What if he had waited until he was more financially stable? What if he had put off such plans until after reaching financial independence?

There are some other pitfalls common on the path of the eldest brother that we must remain aware of. The more success one achieves, the more the risk of falling prey to extreme behaviors. In Chapter 1, we discussed the hedonic treadmill and its twin cousin, overdrive. Saving and money-making can become so addictive that we may find ourselves spinning our wheels rapidly but getting nowhere. Sometimes repeated success in moneymaking can lead us to forget the importance of slowing down and using our money to live a little. Not only the large expenses but also even everyday spending can become problematic.

Frugality is a perfect example. Living on less, maximizing our resources, and a do-it-yourself attitude can indeed supercharge your journey to financial security and wealth. But it is also possible to take these concepts too far.

Have you seen the lengths people are willing to go to save a buck?

I once read a post in a popular financial independence Facebook group about a couple who, while on vacation, bought a loaf of bread and used the iron in their hotel room to make toast. They trumpeted this achievement as evidence that you don't have to spend outrageous sums on food when out of town. These types of tactics cross over to deprivation as opposed to demonstrating reasonable economic choices. Frugality can cheapen the here and now. One has to be clear-sighted about what deprivation looks like in one's life and avoid it assiduously. Smart money management doesn't have to be painful. There is enough unnecessary spending to be cut.

Minimalism has also become exceedingly popular with those who follow the path of the eldest brother. The concept of ridding yourself of unnecessary junk and clutter sounds very appealing. But it's important to understand that the core of such philosophies is the basic idea of simplicity. I think we confound having less with making life easier and more manageable. Getting rid of everything won't fix all or even any of our problems. It won't bring us any closer to understanding our unique purpose, identity, and connections.

HIGH INCOME, BROKE ANYWAY

A word of caution: just because a person makes a high income early in their career doesn't mean that they automatically are following the road of the eldest brother. Front-loading the sacrifice requires not only a significant amount of fuel up front, but also a wise and judicious use of that fuel throughout the journey.

While earning a lot of money will energize your trajectory, it is no guarantee that you will become either wealthy or financially independent; you still have to do the hard work. In my career as a physician, I can think of several high-earning individuals I have encountered who are nothing short of broke. They are buried in debt and one payment away from having their house of cards crumble at their feet.

Sherry was proud of her successful plastic surgery practice. She had built her business from the ground up and felt every bit entitled to the half-million-dollar salary that she was able to squeeze out of the monthly receipts. She bought for her family all the trappings of the upper-class neighborhood that she settled in. In doing so, she lived well above her means; she was mortgaged to the hilt. Her three children went to the most expensive private schools. They summered at the elite summer camps, which they attended sporting the most expensive and fashionable gear. She had all the appearances of wealth, but if you took a look at her financials, you would know that she was actually broke. Sherry's savings rate was a whopping negative 10 percent. She borrowed ten percent above her income each year through credit cards, home equity lines, and personal loans. She had no investments nor fully owned real estate. Her net worth was in the gutter.

How do you think she supported this lifestyle?

Her favorite method was to extract cash from the practice the minute it was recorded in the books. She often had the accountant cut her own payroll checks early, while delaying her employee's biweekly wages. And when the foundation started to crack, she called the local bank and extended her line of credit.

Eventually she had to take a loan against her own 401(k) account, raid her children's college fund, and borrow money from her office manager, who was making a tenth of Sherry's take-home pay. The loan was for a thousand dollars to cover her children's nanny.

She always seemed to find a way to make ends meet until the day she finally couldn't. A routine mammogram showed a breast lump that was eventually diagnosed as cancer. Surgery and chemotherapy required a full month of unexpected and unpaid leave. Her long-term disability policy coverage started only after ninety days, leaving Sherry with little to pay herself.

With no source of income and ever-increasing personal and business debt, Sherry closed her practice and filed for bankruptcy. While she was fortunate that her cancer was ultimately treatable and she didn't become one of my hospice patients, her story is a warning about the dangers of overspending and keeping up with the Joneses. A high income is not the same as a high net worth.

* * *

The financial independence movement has evolved a lot in the aftermath of the Great Recession. The old guard was more interested in accumulating income-producing assets and exiting the workplace as soon as possible. The path of the eldest brother was simply known as "the path"; there were few viable alternatives.

A new generation of financial independence seekers is evolving and challenging the traditional dogma. Whereas the older generation were more enamored of net worth, many younger participants are much less interested in sacrifice; grinding it out for decades in the workplace does not appeal to them. They want to enjoy today and not some imagined nirvana far off in the future. They grew up seeing the benefits of the YOLO lifestyle.

For them, the roads of the middle and youngest brothers are much more appealing.

CHOICE 2: PASSIVE INCOME AND SIDE HUSTLES

Middle brothers choose to define financial independence as a state in which passive income streams and side hustles create enough revenue to cover daily needs. Instead of employing savings and compounding investments, this technique is much more heavily based on either real estate or entrepreneurship.

> **TERMS**
>
> A **side hustle** is a means of making money alongside one's main form of employment or income.

Often, a middle brother starts their career in a typical job—professional or otherwise. Unlike the average employee, however, nights and weekends are spent building side hustles. Although they require a huge amount of work in the beginning, these ventures often become passive over time. As side hustles build and revenues grow, residual income often overtakes W-2 wages.

Why continue to be an employee?

Shalini was a real-estate baron. Over years of working as a residential realtor, she developed the skills and knowledge necessary to build her own passive income stream through investing in commercial real estate. Although she had been accumulating extra savings for years, she was pushed to buy her first investment property after being diagnosed with multiple sclerosis (a debilitating neurological disease that often leads to disability over decades). The process of building multiple income streams became all the more important with the knowledge that she might not have the physical strength required to serve her clients in the future. That way, if she lost her job or her health deteriorated, she would continue to have a viable source of income each month.

Leaving her job as a residential realtor was an unexpected bonus. Although her accounts were almost completely drained at first to acquire new properties, there was a continuous stream of monthly income that provided for an even more extravagant lifestyle than before. Freed from the constraints of a traditional nine-to-five, she was also able to spend more time taking care of herself, doing physical therapy to avoid musculoskeletal issues, and traveling while she was still healthy.

When her multiple sclerosis eventually became debilitating, she hired a property manager to handle the day-to-day decisions. Although the monthly paychecks couldn't allay the devastating changes in her health, the residual income provided comfort during her last years.

Like Shalini, real-estate investors offer a prime example of utilizing the path of the middle brother; they accumulate property and support themselves with rental income. Not only do they have a monthly paycheck requiring little maintenance, but they also can take advantage of several quirks in the tax code to boost profits.

Other examples of middle brothers include bloggers, podcasters, digital entrepreneurs, and YouTube and social media sensations.

While the obvious benefit of this method is that time spent trapped in a cubicle is minimized, it would be a mistake to say that sacrifice becomes completely foreign. Creating passive income streams is incredibly hard work in the beginning. Side hustles can be frustrating and feel like a waste of time; many are unsuccessful. Aligning one's purpose, identity, and connections with these extracurricular activities can allay some of these feelings. The daily grind is much more bearable if done for one's own benefit and not for some faceless boss or corporation.

WORTH VERSUS WORTH IT

Grumpus Maximus (a pseudonym), in his book *The Golden Albatross*, introduces the concept of "worth versus worth it."[21] While he uses this decision framework to calculate whether the value of a pension is worth extending one's military career, the calculus when it comes to passive income and side hustles is basically similar.

As we will discuss in Chapter 7, our available time on this earth is constant and unchangeable. How we spend it, however, is completely up to us. Do we really want to create even more work for ourselves? Do we want to fill all of our waking hours outside of the nine-to-five trying to build these passive income streams?

The example of Shalini, our real-estate investor with multiple sclerosis, helps clarify some of these issues. She pivoted from being a residential realtor to owning a side hustle and leasing commercial properties. For her, the extra time and energy were well worth the reward of eventually living on passive income. Success, however, didn't come immediately.

Shalini's original plan had been to buy and flip houses. Six months into her first project, she was ready to throw in the towel. She was deeply in debt, behind schedule, and couldn't concentrate on her day job. For her, it became abundantly clear that this was not going to be a successful endeavor. The *worth* of her house-flipping business just wasn't *worth it*; the money she made did not compensate for the extra pain and frustration.

---

21 Grumpus Maximus, *The Golden Albatross: How to Determine If Your Pension Is Worth It* (Glen Allen, VA: ChooseFI Media, 2020).

Her second venture, commercial real estate, was a completely different story.

Before you jump into the role of the middle brother and begin your pursuit of side hustles, consider Shalini's example. Is the value and income created worth the worry and hassles that go along with starting a new business?

Ultimately, if you hope to follow the path of the middle brother, your goal should be to answer this question for yourself and your family. Regardless of the moniker, passive income, especially in the beginning, feels anything but passive. In fact, maybe we should change the name!

IS PASSIVE INCOME REALLY PASSIVE?

We love to use the term "passive income." It is the calling card of the financial independence community. The idea is to build a perpetual money machine over a short period of time, and then reap the benefits for decades to come; it sounds almost too good to be true—which should immediately set off alarms. Although many of us have grown up believing there is no such thing as a free lunch, we somehow hope that this situation is different.

Is the childhood saying right, or could passive income truly be passive?

I'm not denying the existence of side gigs, hustles, and investments that can sustain a healthy lifestyle. The more salient question is how much time should we expect to spend on maintenance. Passive income that requires countless hours of nurturing is no longer passive; for all intents and purposes, it's a W-2 job—one in which you have wrestled all the responsibilities and liabilities from a third party and placed them squarely on yourself.

In these situations, I like to think in terms of a relative passivity index. Some money machines require more maintenance than others. Winning the lottery or receiving a family inheritance creates truly passive income. Those events require almost no work and immediately propel one into financial stability, a shortcut to the path of the eldest brother.

They are also fairly unreliable.

The stock market scores almost as high on the relative passivity index. This is the front-loaded path, in which one accumulates cash, invests it, and then lives off the proceeds (as we discussed in the last section). After a certain amount of reading and education, your average portfolio will take merely hours a month to maintain.

The tables turn completely with real estate, small businesses, blogs, online web stores, or other forms of digital entrepreneurship. These endeavors can require a large investment of time and may create as much anxiety and stress as any ballyhooed W-2. No matter how often we refer to Tim Ferriss's four-hour work week, for the majority, it will never come to pass.[22]

I often hear this same sentiment expressed by the highly successful real-estate investors, online sales experts earning six figures, and million-dollar bloggers I interview on the *Earn & Invest* podcast. They fought for their income with blood, sweat, and tears long before we were able to recognize their current success.

We make a grievous mistake when we view a person's ending and assume that the journey was passive from the start. Ironically, the trick to being truly passive is our good old friend: front-loading. What we like to call passive income streams are actually front-loaded businesses that now have been placed on autopilot.

For these reasons, I believe we should eventually abandon the concept of *passive income* and replace it with *residual income*, a far more accurate descriptor. Real-estate investors spend years accumulating knowledge, buying and managing properties, and setting up systems before they move into a more passive role. Business owners, consultants, and book writers often work long hours aggressively pursuing their short-term goals to assure success.

Passive income, in the most absolute sense, may not truly exist. Whether you are an eldest brother who invested money in the stock market or a

22 Tim Ferriss, *The 4-Hour Work Week: Escape 9–5, Live Anywhere, and Join the New Rich* (New York: Crown Publishers, 2009).

middle brother who ventures into side hustles, you are going to have to do the work. As the old adage goes, nothing is for free.

Besides the fact that passive income streams can be work-intensive, we must also be aware that they carry a certain amount of inherent risk. I have experienced this phenomenon many times as a landlord. My rental properties have suffered through cockroaches, rats, and even noisy neighbors that made my units unrentable. I have spent thousands of dollars on unexpected fixes, such as the time a heating unit needed to be replaced or the period that my properties remained vacant due to the COVID-19 pandemic. If you are a small business entrepreneur, you may be one natural disaster, housing glut, or change in a YouTube algorithm away from being back in the job market.

For this reason, the path of the middle brother is suited for risk-takers and entrepreneurs, free spirits, and those who think beyond traditional employment and aren't security-motivated. This should be your choice if you are better at working for yourself than for others.

CHOICE 3: THE PASSION PLAY

People who follow the path of the youngest brother have no interest in grinding it out. They figure they can climb all the way up Maslow's pyramid while simultaneously pursuing enriching employment. If their job both provides ample cash to cover basic needs as well as fulfills a sense of purpose, identity, and connections, then there is no need to wait on compounding interest. I call this approach "the passion play."

Recognizing the passion play as a viable path is the most controversial choice an expert can make. In a sense, I include this approach to totally redefine financial independence: instead of focusing on a net worth goal or a monthly income, this technique defines financial independence as "the ability to fill one's time primarily with meaningful activities—while also making enough money to survive." Since we will be performing some sort of work our whole lives (whether for money or for ourselves), why not spend our time doing something we love and getting paid for it?

Remember Bobbie, whom you met in the Introduction? His love for big trucks provided a career full of passion and excitement. He couldn't wait to get into the office every morning and scour the trade pages for the latest new additions to the market. His biggest regret in the dying process was his inability to sustain his previous work activities. He rarely worried about money because his beloved business always provided enough.

Bobbie had neither the patience to front-load the sacrifice and accumulate assets as the driver of independence nor the inclination to build passive income streams to provide monthly revenue as the conduit to financial freedom. Like all youngest brothers pursuing the passion play, he used the most basic resource he had available: human capital. He invested his time and energy and imbued his work with sweat equity.

And it brought him joy.

THE JOY OF WORK

Some would have called Angel lucky; others would strongly disagree. He dropped out of college and found part-time work in his uncle's antique shop. He spent his days refurbishing damaged furniture and chatting amiably with customers. One morning, a teenager walked in and offered a few dollars for an odd assortment of baseball cards left over from a recent buy. The kid—who would eventually become Angel's first employee—then pulled out a price guide and valued the collection at double what he had just bought it for.

Angel was enthralled.

Over the next few months, he bought and sold baseball cards, and his unexpected success allowed him to acquire his uncle's business. The small antique shop became a hub for neighborhood kids to purchase, sell, and trade cards. Angel spent the next few decades mentoring teenagers as they frequented his shop. The cash flow was steady and provided for his wife and growing daughter; there wasn't much extra, but there was enough.

Angel loved his life and work.

After being admitted to hospice with pancreatic cancer, he was unable to keep the shop afloat. It turns out Angel himself was just as much of a draw as were the baseball cards. He died shortly thereafter, never wanting for anything but what he already had. His wife mourned his passing; I remember the tears falling down her face as her mouth couldn't help but curl into a half smile: "He loved those cards! Boy, did he love those cards."

Angel and Bobbie both lived by a motto that I am sure you have heard before: *if you do something you love you will never have to work a day in your life.*

While many youngest brothers are prime examples of this axiom, it is unwise to automatically assume everyone will have this luxury. In fact, I believe the opposite is true. Very few will be able to turn their passions into a full-time job.

Does that mean the path of the youngest brother is untenable?

While I have met many Angels and Bobbies during my tenure as a hospice doctor, the number seems to be decreasing every year. Although I wouldn't discount this path altogether, the difficulties of the passion play become clear as we examine a myth which might be one of the most destructive forces in the workplace today.

THE "LABOR OF LOVE" MYTH

Making a living at what you love is incredibly difficult. This idea—that love is an integral part of work, called the "labor of love" myth—has permeated American culture over the past few decades. And for good reason. We are spending more time and energy on the job than ever before. Our nights and weekends are often interrupted by the interminable buzzing of our mobile phones alerting that we have received a new email. Employment has become a much bigger part of our lives; we had better learn to enjoy it.

While the theory sounds quite appealing, many are finding that "work will never love us back." It is highly unlikely that we will always enjoy every aspect of our nine-to-five, all our coworkers, or every project. Our jobs will invariably require us to forgo activities we would rather be engaged in from time to time; there will always be frustration.

As society encourages us to do what we love for a living, we are seeing rising levels of burnout, stagnant wages, and a decline in work-life balance. Many feel disappointed when they either can't find employment they are passionate about or, conversely, can't earn an adequate living when they do.

Even if you are cognizant of what type of work brings you joy, there are still several hurdles. For one, failure can be devastating. Just as Angel was diagnosed with pancreatic cancer, the Major League Baseball strike during the 1994–95 season caused the baseball card market to crash. I remember Angel's distress as he struggled to unload product even as he was becoming more ill from chemotherapy.

There is also the havoc that being passionate about work can create at home. Bobbie often missed dinner with his wife in order to hang around the shop and receive new truck deliveries during odd hours. Her death, which preceded his by a few years, was even more traumatic in light of all the time they had spent away from each other.

Being married to work leaves less room for relationships and the deeper connections that fulfill us. Youngest brothers often struggle between these competing demands, and they tend to fail at both of them.

Angel and I shared one grim habit that still haunts me to this day. We both passed up vacations and joyous experiences because we were afraid to leave our jobs behind. For him, it was the shop; for me, my busy practice. Angel often voiced this regret during his last days. He regretted that his passion didn't always extend outside the four confining walls of his store.

The other risk of turning what you love into a profession is that you might grow to hate your passion over time. Receiving external rewards for things we are internally motivated to do can be disastrous.

The burnout I suffered during my medical training is an especially common issue with physicians but can also be seen with other civic-minded professions like teachers and police officers. In contrast to those who experience the dangers associated with the "labor of love" myth, these professionals do not develop hatred for their jobs. Instead, they suffer from something that has recently been defined as moral injury.[23] They are continuously asked to make decisions based not on what they think is best, but rather on what has become most expedient in their given fields.

Cyrus, the teacher turned college counselor from Chapter 3, was facing similar issues. With the many changes in his school's math curriculum, he could no longer teach using methods he thought were most appropriate. His pension, however, made it difficult to extract himself from a profession that no longer fed his soul. His fiscal vulnerability made leaving all but impossible. He felt lucky to have the ability to pivot midcareer toward counseling and coaching. Many don't have that option.

There are several other roadblocks to those building a career focused on the passion play. Of all the brothers, the youngest are the most naive about money and material wealth; the fulfillment they receive from work is expected to be *enough*. While enticing at first, there are several consequences from such thinking.

Lack of material reserves can be devastating when you become a victim of the unexpected. This can range from losing interest and passion in one's work, as previously discussed, to suffering an injury on the job and becoming unable to perform critical duties. Although a good disability policy (discussed in the next chapter) can mitigate the issue of injury, there is little that can be done for passion fatigue. For so many of the doctors with whom I have worked, overwhelming student loan debt severely hampers their ability to leave, even after their interest in the profession has begun to wane.

Avoiding the risks of the youngest brother takes a mix of good advice, the right insurance, long-term planning, and the recognition that even dream jobs will not completely fulfill our needs for purpose, identity, and connections; we also require people and experiences.

Barring these concerns, the path of the youngest brother can be especially great for dreamers, free spirits, musicians, and artists. The older brothers

---

23   Andrew Jameton, *Nursing Practice: The Ethical Issues* (Englewood Cliffs, NJ: Prentice Hall, 1984).

are often envious, because money no longer appears to be the driver of their youngest brother's daily activities.

Doesn't that sound nice?

I CHOSE TO FRONT-LOAD

When it came to my path to financial independence, I never considered anything other than the path of the eldest brother and front-loading. I was born to two highly skilled professionals who together held multiple advanced degrees. We grew up with the expectation of achieving higher education and learning a life skill. The idea of leaving college or graduate school without a clearly defined professional pathway was never even a consideration.

Since my earliest dreams were to be a physician, I, in a sense, thought I was also following the passion play. But from the very beginning of my career, I realized that passion wouldn't sustain me in the long run, and burnout was a more likely probability. So I dedicated myself to a demanding position that required countless nights and weekends. There were no second thoughts or disturbing concerns that maybe there was a more humane method to reach my goals. I even doubled down and used my professional skills to partake in several side hustles for extra cash. I became obsessed with the idea of creating wealth in as little time as possible.

Simultaneously, I began to realize that writing, public speaking, and other forms of communicating were much more in line with my true sense of meaning and purpose. I dipped my toe cautiously into these activities but refused to dive in the deep end; I never considered trying to monetize these efforts. I separated money and passion as if they were oil and water. I told myself that medicine was for making money, and communicating was for joy.

Was I wrong?

My viewpoint was very representative not only of my upbringing, but also that of my generation. For me as a member of Generation X, the idea of sacrifice in the workplace was not exactly foreign. In some ways, I believe the millennials and Gen Zers have a much better relationship with work-life balance. They have less fear when it comes to following their passions.

It's difficult to play the Monday morning quarterback with such complicated decisions. I'm not sure I can definitively say that I would have done things differently if I had the chance to start again. While being a doctor certainly brought about some uncomfortable moments, it wasn't all bad. The skills I gained in medical school and residency allowed me to profoundly affect other people's lives. This was an utter privilege.

I have also greatly benefited from the economic stability that wouldn't have been possible without medicine. I was able to stock the coffers for all those years, invest, and build a stable financial plan that would withstand the test of time. Unlike those who rely on passive income or a passion-related profession, I believe my finances are much more resilient; I am generating revenue through preexisting assets (stocks and bonds). Even if those assets stop making extra money, I still own them.

They have value.

I personally found that building other passive income streams and side hustles was a difficult proposition that often led to much work but lower returns than I had hoped for.

I also have thought long and hard about whether I would have been happy as the youngest brother pursuing the passion play instead of going to medical school. I could have dedicated my life to becoming a writer, radio personality, or public speaker. While this sounds wonderful at first, we often forget, while strolling through daydream land, that being passionate does not automatically ensure a solid income.

What if I wasn't good enough to support myself with creativity?

An overlooked benefit of the traditional path to financial independence is that after retiring, one can pursue passion without reservations. You can revel in the process and dispatch of all fears regarding the outcome. You can fail fabulously without consequence.

I didn't want the stress of making a living to impinge on pursuing my passion; I was afraid that it would start to feel like any other job. Front-loading was right for me, but it isn't for everyone.

Some feel the urgency of now so acutely that the idea of sacrifice becomes anathema. These are people who quail at the idea of grinding it out in a desk from nine to five each day. For them, passive income or the passion play just might be the answer.

YOU DON'T HAVE TO DECIDE BETWEEN MONEY AND PASSION

Although we have further defined the archetypes of the three brothers in the previous sections, reality is a lot more complicated. There are thousands of roads in which both wealth and passion may even intersect. We often forget that we may jump from one road to another at various times in our life or careers. We don't have to choose between money and passion, sacrifice and joy, in the long term.

We may, as the situation calls for, tactically decide to delay gratification in the short term—embrace the suck for a defined period of time in order to reap the financial benefits of sacrifice.

> **TERMS**
>
> **Embrace the suck:** This military term means to consciously accept or appreciate something that is extremely unpleasant but unavoidable for forward progress.

Or we might bring our financial goals to a screeching halt and turn off the road for a passion play. The possibilities are endless. The point is to navigate this maze of choice with intention and clear goals in mind.

We can replace "either-or" with "both-and."

Many choose to front-load the sacrifice and build wealth when they are young and energetic, able to put in long hours at a job that might not be personally fulfilling but that generates a high income. Later, when on more stable financial ground, they accept a significant decrease in pay to pursue a job that allows them to explore their passions. They can transition back and forth as needed. And the layered approach of the middle brother should not be discounted either. During my early days as an attending physician, I started a business selling artwork online. This not only provided passive income, but also was something I was passionate about and could do in concert with my W-2 employment.

The dying have taught me to be intentional and thoughtful about the process. To pay homage to the urgency of now as well as plan for the future. Ultimately, emotional well-being and self-actualization have to be built in tandem with wealth, not in a hierarchical fashion. You don't want to wait until you have a terminal illness to finally embrace the things that are most important to you.

To say that you can only have money or passion is a false dichotomy—a dichotomy that I only now realize could have cost me dearly.

If I had died at the age of forty, as my father had, I would have missed out on so much: the joy of nervously standing in front of a packed auditorium right before giving a speech, and the exhilaration of a microphone perched in front of my face as I start a podcast episode. I would be another one of Bronnie Ware's survey subjects.

> I wish I had lived a life truer to myself.
>
> I wish I hadn't worked so hard.
>
> I wish I had let myself be happier.

To avoid this trap, we have to be more intentional about weighing the positives and negatives of each brother's path now. That's why, in the next chapter, we'll start to put your financial house in order today so that you'll be prepared no matter how many or few tomorrows you have in front of you.

THE PARABLE OF THREE BROTHERS: WHICH BROTHER ARE YOU?

1. Clear your schedule for an hour for two to three separate days over the next week. During that time, make sure all electronics are turned to silent, you are well-rested and fed, and you have found a quiet, comfortable place to concentrate.

2. Imagine that you have just graduated college and have secured your dream job. Your family and loved ones are overjoyed. What would you be doing?

3. What aspects of this new job would be most gratifying? Would it be the joy in the moment-to-moment work? The freedom of self-determination and an open schedule? The ability to progress toward leadership? How much money are you making?

4. Make a list of the things that you love about this new job and rank them in order of importance. Be specific here; make sure you recognize which characteristics make this job a perfect fit for you. Are you self-employed or working for someone else? Take your time and be thoughtful. It might take a few days to complete this list.

5. Now create this same list for your current job. How does it match up to the imaginary one? Are you surprised at how dissimilar the lists are? If so, don't worry. Often our imaginary dream jobs are idealized versions of reality.

6. Now try to figure out which brother's path is most in line with your wish list. Eldest brothers will value a high salary and quick promotions but worry less about enjoying their daily tasks.

7. Are you a middle brother? Highly self-motivated, they value an open schedule and feel trapped and confined by an oppressive work environment. They often don't like being told what to do.

Does real estate or entrepreneurship sound enticing?

8. Do you identify with the youngest brother? You are passionate about what you do and would continue even if you weren't being paid. You are likely creative—a musician or an artist.

9. Finally, apply what you have learned about these paths to evaluate your own work environment. Could you be happier in a different job? Are you taking a path that does not suit you?

10. Although up to this point we have been discussing work, you'll see that these concepts apply to goals, dreams, and relationships also.

CHAPTER 5

PUTTING YOUR FINANCIAL HOUSE IN ORDER

You are going to die.

Imagine that I have walked into your hospital room and have gently sat down in the chair besides you. If you are married, your husband or wife listens intently by your side. Maybe a parent or sibling is also present.

I have reviewed the CAT scans, spoken to the specialists, and studied the labs. There are many possible treatments that could be offered, but I fear they will not stem the course of all that is happening already. The tumor is too advanced—the metastases, too malignant.

You pause and struggle to take a deep breath. You were aware that the hospice team had been called but are only now coming to terms with the true meaning of this consult. You look frantically into your spouse's eyes and see your own pain and fear reflected back at you. You both thought that you had more time.

Let me explain. In my experience, every person, young and old, healthy and diseased, wakes up each morning with a plan for the day...I do not know when you are going to die. Doctors are poor at estimating such things. But I would like to help you focus on the life each day occurring around you. Death is a period at the end of a sentence, not a set of parentheses or quotation marks.

Your life flashes in front of you—right there in that moment. You contemplate all that you have accomplished and that at which you have failed. The names and the faces of your loved ones quickly flit through your mind as you consider your legacy. What mistakes have you made, both financially and otherwise? A question weighs heavily on your mind: *Am I ready to die?*

Well? Are you?

Whether you like it or not, you are dying. Maybe not the way described in this scenario. Maybe not today. Maybe not tomorrow. Death occurs just once for each of us, but you are dying from the day you are born, and by the time you get around to reading this book, you might have already lived quite a bit of life. These questions are not meant to be morbid nor disturbing, but often we must be rocked out of our sense of complacency to make meaningful change.

Only you will be able to determine whether you have lived a life consistent with your own unique purpose, identity, and connections. But having your financial house in order will go far in giving you the space, time, and freedom to pursue that which is most meaningful to you. It will also help you parse out the paths of each of the three brothers in your own life and use their wisdom to guide your financial decisions.

Much as in Chapter 3, where we defined the dichotomy between YOLO and deferred gratification in terms of opportunity cost, shoring up our own finances and legacy means coming to terms with another dichotomy, which centers on two basic fears when it comes to dying and money.

We are either afraid that we will die too soon and never enjoy what we have labored to accomplish, or that we will die far off in the future and not have enough money to sustain our needs: we'll die broke.

WHAT SCARES YOU MORE?

My father always knew that he was going to die young. In fact, he expressed this exact sentiment to my mother before she agreed to marry him. Whether he was conscious of it or not, I believe many of his decisions were colored by this belief, especially when it came to his career. After finishing his fellowship in oncology, he was offered a lucrative job in private practice that would have far exceeded the pay that he would be able to make in an academic position. Yet he turned down this opportunity to maintain employment in the Veterans Affairs hospital at Northwestern University. While the pay was obviously much less, the position allowed him to work with all the intellectual rigor but none of the time and emotional commitment required in private practice.

My father was a tinkerer. He had a small utility room in the basement filled with tools and other supplies and spent countless hours building and creating. He was an avid photographer and used a spare closet to develop his own photos. He was even in the midst of learning Hebrew when he died suddenly of a brain aneurysm.

My father understood the urgency of now, and it is clear to me, in hindsight, that his certainty about dying young allowed him to embrace meaningful pursuits up until the very end of his life. He didn't, however, put much mental energy toward accumulating wealth. As my mother said when I interviewed her for the *Earn & Invest* podcast, "The money was just never there!"

He did, on the other hand, take several steps to mitigate the risk of his own premature mortality and ensure his legacy. He invested in a life insurance policy at a young age that would eventually support our family and provide funding for my college and medical school education. He also suggested that my mother go back to school; instead of returning to a PhD program in organic chemistry that she had started but never finished decades earlier, he encouraged her to get an MBA from Kellogg University. His words ring hauntingly true, even today: "You want to have a career that provides enough income in case something happens to me."

My father died a few months before my mom ascended to the podium and received her diploma as a newly minted CPA. By that time, she had already been offered a position at a Big Four accounting firm.

Was it good luck or wise preparation?

Unlike my dad, I grew up with very different feelings about my own longevity. I have always believed that I would live to a ripe old age. This belief has colored my approach to career and finances. In many ways, I was able to delay my passions in order to build the appropriate amount of jet fuel to power my transatlantic flight. The urgency of now was replaced with a wholehearted wish to delay gratification now to benefit the future. My biggest fear was not dying prematurely, but rather having inadequate assets to provide for myself and my family for an extended period of retirement.

Getting your financial house in order requires understanding a few basic personal finance concepts (which we will discuss below), weighing them carefully based on which brother's path you most identify with, and coming to terms with what scares you most (dying too soon or dying poor). Armed with this knowledge, you can create a financial plan that balances the urgency of now and your wealth needs for the future. After all, most of us are not as certain as my father was about when our time will be up.

KNOW YOUR NET WORTH

Any good GPS system requires two data points to fulfill its purpose: a starting point and a final destination. Although you may have a clear idea of your intended destination, how much thought have you put into defining where you currently stand? Do you know your net worth?

> **TERMS**
>
> **Net worth** is the total wealth of an individual, company, or household, taking account of all financial assets and liabilities.

Believe it or not, most people have no idea what they own and what they owe. They see their finances as an amorphous blob and have no systematic method to evaluate where they stand. Regardless of which brother's path you decide to follow, a little bit of clarity about your actual financial situation is needed.

We have talked about net worth in vague terms up to this point, but it makes sense to spend a few paragraphs explaining how and why it's time to get more granular. Let's start with a definition.

Most simply, your net worth is an accounting of all your assets and liabilities. It's calculated by tabulating everything of value that you either own or owe: cash, property, possessions, investments, debts, and so on (figure 4).

ASSETS − LIABILITIES = NET WORTH

ASSETS	LIABILITIES
Checking accounts	Consumer debt
Savings accounts	Personal loans
Retirement savings	Student loans
Real estate	Mortgage
Autos	Auto loans
	Other debt

Figure 4. Net worth

The first step is to write out all the things you own that have value (assets).

A list of common assets used in this calculation can be seen in figure 4. Perfect is the enemy of good here—you do not have to include less valuable items like clothes and perishable goods.

Next, what are your liabilities? This is money that you currently owe. Some examples include consumer debts, student loans, mortgages, and auto loans. Your net worth is then calculated by subtracting your assets from your liabilities. It is that simple.

If the number you come up with is greater than zero, congratulations! You have a positive net worth. You have more than you owe. If your number falls below zero, no reason to despair, it just means that you have some more work to do. In fact, a negative net worth is fairly common for younger people due, in part, to home ownership and educational debt. While having a negative net worth is not ideal, houses are usually appreciating assets (go up in value over time). We leverage a small amount of money to own something of greater value that may eventually be worth more. This is not always a bad thing.

Now that you have calculated your net worth, you can make an honest appraisal of where you are—your starting point. This is important. Most people are completely unaware of where they stand financially. They think that blissful ignorance will somehow save them from dealing with the emotional stress of financial hardship.

This lack of awareness sounds oddly similar to how most people approach the dying process. At first, they will do just about anything to avoid facing reality. Once this hurdle is overcome, however, it is far easier to decide what they want the rest of their journey to look like.

Knowing your net worth is essential regardless of what scares you most. If dying young is your biggest fear, having a good accounting of your current resources or the debt you may saddle your loved ones with can be extremely helpful in deciding how much money is available for your current opportunity fund (the YOLO fund we discussed in Chapter 3).

Ask Shalini, our real-estate baron from the last chapter. Understanding and building a positive net worth, combined with her knowledge of a shortened life span due to multiple sclerosis, allowed her to take maximal advantage of the monthly income she received from her thriving passive income streams. She jumped on the opportunity to travel throughout Asia while she still had the strength and energy, but she also set up a college fund for her two beloved nieces. There was no need to worry about saving for a retirement that would last for decades.

For those who see longevity in their future, this calculation marks the entry point on your road to financial independence. And happily, that destination is rather easy to define using a few basic calculations.

MIND THE GAP

Your ability to save in excess of what you earn is the most obvious as well as the best kept secret to a successful financial life. You simply have to learn how to mind the gap.

Money Earned – Money Spent = The Savings Gap

By examining this equation closely, you might feel that earnings and spending are of equal importance. The truth, however, is a little more complicated; they both have their shortcomings. Earning extra money is limited in the sense that we take home only a fraction of every paycheck depending on what tax bracket those dollars belong to. Uncle Sam always gets his cut. Unlike money earned, savings (money not spent) can never be unlimited; only so much blood can be squeezed from a stone. Savings are, however, immune from the drag of taxes. When you choose not to spend $100, you get the benefit of having the whole $100 left over. When you earn an extra $100, at least a third of it may be owed to the government.

How powerful is saving in your path to financial independence and possibly early retirement? Pete Adeney, also known as Mr. Money Mustache and a prime example of an eldest brother, calculated the years to retirement for a given household based on savings rate (defined as percentage of take-home pay saved and invested with 5 percent returns). The graph shown in figure 5 is what he came up with. The results are shocking: increasing one's savings rate by as little as 5 percent can shave off years in the journey to retirement!

SAVINGS RATE (PERCENT)	WORKING YEARS UNTIL RETIREMENT
5	66
10	51
15	43
20	37
25	32
30	28
35	25
40	22
45	19
50	17
55	14.5
60	12.5
65	10.5
70	8.5
75	7
80	5.3
85	4
90	Under 3
95	Under 2
100	Zero

Figure 5. Working years until retirement
(courtesy of mrmoneymustache.com)

Mr. Money Mustache's calculations and net worth assumptions are based on the 4 percent safe withdrawal rate that we will discuss momentarily. The specific amount of money earned is not nearly as important as the percentage of savings.

It goes without saying that as you modify your budget appropriately and start to mind the gap, you will accumulate excess cash. What you do with that excess cash is very much related to your fears about longevity. My father, knowing he was going to die young, chose to use the savings gap to enjoy what he saw as a limited time on earth. This was a very reasonable decision for him to make, and ended up producing meaningful returns. I, on the other hand, was squirreling away resources and building assets towards the ultimate goal of a perpetual money machine.

THE PERPETUAL MONEY MACHINE

As our ideas of financial independence have evolved, so have the variations on the three approaches I've shared in the previous chapter. While those who see their time as limited are more interested in funding the here and now, those who dream of longevity have to take a much different approach to long-term wealth. If you build a perpetual money machine, the cash will come. But there is no way around it: you have to build it. Here is where the real work comes in. The specifics will vary depending on your style, but every path to financial independence must focus on three areas:

TERMS

Earn: Front-load the sacrifice so you can let both earnings and experience compound, develop passive income that can sustain you over the long term, or go for a passion play.

Save: Use frugality as a tool when it serves, and make it a lifestyle, if necessary.

Invest: Squirrel that money away in a diversified portfolio of asset classes. When it comes to stock, choose high-quality low-cost indexes and develop a good sense of apathy toward the short-term ups and downs of the market.

Then dig in—for years. Put your head down and work. With a little bit of luck and time, you will look up one day and your perpetual money machine will be humming along. And you'll have choices about how to spend your time.

The good life was never really about financial independence. Financial independence is a superpower that allows you to pursue long-term contentment unburdened by the bonds of fiscal responsibility. So, take the steps to build your own perpetual money machine, schedule occasional maintenance, and find better things to do with your time.

For eldest brothers in particular, the journey begins with the 4 percent rule.

THE 4 PERCENT RULE

The most difficult concept for a newly minted eldest brother to grasp regarding their financial independence number is the variability. The reasonableness of our projections relies heavily on something most financial independence novices have never done before: create a budget. How much you need to save and invest is directly impacted by how much you want to spend.

It is easier than ever to track spending. A number of free programs are available, provided by companies like Mint and Personal Capital. Or, if you prefer more functionality, there are paid programs that are rather inexpensive and well worth the cost, such as YNAB (You Need a Budget). And, of course, there is always good old pencil and paper or a spreadsheet. Any of these options will suffice.

Once you have tabulated your average monthly and yearly spending, it is a simple calculation to determine how much you need in investable assets to provide for yourself for the rest of your life without ever working again.

The safe withdrawal rate has been studied quite a bit. This is the percentage of your total invested assets that you can afford to liquidate every year and still not run out of money. These calculations assume that your money is actively invested in stocks and bonds and accruing average annual returns.

The 4 percent rule of thumb is generally the accepted standard. It is based on the Trinity Study published in 1998, in which the authors looked at all thirty-year periods between 1925 and 1995 using historical stock market data.[24] They found 4 percent to be the optimal safe withdrawal rate for a thirty-year retirement.

Another way of saying this is that you need a nest egg of twenty-five times your yearly spending. So if you live on $40,000 a year, you will need to accumulate and invest $1 million (either $40,000 x 25 = $1 million total or $1,000,000 x .04=$40,000 per year).

Since 1998, however, several researchers and renowned economists have adjusted this percentage up or down by as much as 0.5 percent. The exact percentage has varied based on a number of reasonable critiques of the 4 percent rule that we will discuss next.

Most important for early retirees is that invested assets may need to survive much more than thirty years. These longer duration portfolios are especially at risk if a severe downturn comes to pass within the first ten years after retirement. This phenomenon, called sequence of returns

---

24   P. L. Cooley, C. M. Hubbard, and D. T. Walz, "Retirement Savings: Choosing a Withdrawal Rate That Is Sustainable," *AAII Journal* 10, no. 3 (1998): 16–21.

risk, can deplete savings quickly and leave less in assets to compound over time. Other critics point to the danger of a one-size-fits-all formula. Given that possibility of unexpected expenses, health care costs, and common unforeseen issues like divorce, the safe withdrawal calculations aren't as durable as one would hope.

Herb, our expert in geoarbitrage who retired in the 1960s, hit a rough patch in the stock market just a few years into retirement. He watched his net worth drop by almost 50 percent before recovering. His wife remembers several months of careful spending. She even recalls thinking seriously about taking a part-time job at a local grocery market. While their financials recovered, there were other times, such as the Black Monday stock market crash in the late 1980s, that gave them pause.[25]

While Herb's experiences demonstrate that these critiques hold some merit, I still believe that the 4 percent rule is a good rule of a thumb—a foundation to build on and modify based on our own unique situation. Perfect can be the enemy of good enough. We shouldn't let these critiques dissuade us from picking a good ending place.

The perpetual money machines of middle and youngest brothers will look slightly different from the one for the eldest brother. For middle brothers, they will concentrate on building passive income streams that match monthly spending needs. The less maintenance and more durable those passive income streams are, the better. Youngest brothers, on the other hand, will search for a job they love that will pay the monthly bills. When you love your work, it barely feels like work at all!

YOUNGEST BROTHERS AND END OF LIFE

Getting your financial house in order means navigating your own path to financial stability, building a perpetual money machine, and integrating whether your main fear is dying too soon or dying broke. While there are cautionary tales to be told for all the brothers, youngest brothers tend to

---

25   Adam Hays, "Black Monday," *Investopedia*, September 16, 2021.

best exemplify the risks of putting off this issue both economically and otherwise.

I have taken care of many youngest brothers as a hospice physician. They are a powerful reminder of how passion can transform our lives. They tend to die as they lived—with one last truck to sell, poem to write, or baseball card to trade. Their reluctance to leave this earth is much less related to fear and more to a sense of unfinished business.

Because they strived to quench their passions, youngest brothers can experience joyful deaths after a life of fulfillment. Yet it is not uncommon for them to leave a mess behind. Family members lament how they were always competing for attention that they never fully received from the youngest brother. These types can also leave behind a long list of vacations not taken and events not attended. Pursuing one's passion can come at a cost.

The biggest regret of the youngest brothers is that they didn't take the time to slow down, to stop and smell the roses. They never felt the pride of accomplishment or even the finality of a job well done because they were always focused on the next best thing. In the parable, after reaching the end of the road, the youngest brother turns around and walks back the way he came. To deny the natural beginnings and ending in life is not always healthy. Sometimes our paths are too narrow and defined; we may not be aware of the joy that comes with pausing or taking on a new adventure.

Should you really be worrying about baseball cards when you are diagnosed with pancreatic cancer? Angel was. Will you be?

The economic effects can be just as devastating. When the passion play prohibits us from building a stable financial plan, purchasing the right insurance, or building the right team of advisers, disaster lurks around the corner for not only us, but also our families. Youngest brothers are prone to forming poor financial habits. They will always feel too busy to make the proper arrangements.

There are several steps we can take to mitigate these risks and ensure that whichever brother you most identify with, you leave this world and your loved ones with a much stronger legacy.

RISK MITIGATION: THE BEST FINANCIAL PLANS HAVE FOUR LEGS

Now that we have defined some of the basic principles undergirding our perpetual money machines, it is time to put all we have learned together and discuss risk mitigation. We are well on the road to either accumulating wealth and squirreling away our savings into investments or judiciously spending on that which matters most to us. We know whether our biggest fear is dying too soon or living too long—but what if we are wrong? What more can we do to protect our financial futures?

The concept of risk mitigation is one of the most important in personal finance. As with the COVID-19 pandemic, we have no idea what the future will bring. Our inability to accurately read the tea leaves behooves us to take steps to protect ourselves against the natural ups and downs of the market as well as our own financial needs. One of the ways to achieve this piece of mind is to build a financial plan with at least four legs.

Although a key to safe and healthy investing, the nebulous idea of diversification can stifle new investors and personal finance novices. *How much is enough? What qualifies as diversified?* The questions abound. In order to make the concept clearer, I like to look at my financial framework as a tabletop. When it comes to revenue streams, the best financial plans have four legs to ensure stability. Any less and your table is likely to topple over. More than four can add stability but can also lead to overkill.

THE FLAMINGO

The one-legged plan is the most dangerous of all. It is usually based on a single concept: the W-2 wage. Like the flamingo standing atop one leg, it can be toppled over with a single blow.

What does the flamingo financial plan look like?

This is the ride-or-die company man whose only income is his paycheck. His retirement money is tied up in a defined benefit pension. His main stock holdings consist of company shares that he bought at a discount.

This is the most unstable of situations. With all the eggs in one basket, he is one scandal away from bankruptcy, à la Enron.

THE TWO-LEGGER

The two-legger is slightly better, but not much. Take the flamingo just described, but instead of investing only in company stock, the two-legger puts extra cash in a broadly indexed, low-fee mutual fund (and bonds). By adding a touch of diversification, the situation becomes slightly more stable; unlike the plan of the one-legged flamingo, the gentlest of breezes will not topple the two-legger's financial plan.

While slightly better, there are foreseeable problems with this particular allocation mix. A stock market crash that causes our two-legged friend's company to fail will be disastrous. Not only could she be laid off, but she will have to liquidate her slumping portfolio to make ends meet.

THE THREE-LEGGED STOOL

Here is where we are finally approaching stability. If we add real estate holdings to our two-legger, the ability to withstand stress becomes much greater. The three-legged stool is an improvement, but I would still say that the best financial plans have four legs. If your real estate holdings go south, it's like sawing off one leg of the stool. Now you have a highly unstable structure ready to topple over at any time.

THE DINING ROOM TABLE

The dining room table is an American institution. Rightly so—it is the most stable. It's solid and well-built, and often people can rely on this piece of furniture for a lifetime. When we apply this metaphor to revenue streams, this means adding in side hustles to our already multipronged approach:

Leg 1: W-2, company stock, pension

Leg 2: Broadly indexed, low-cost mutual funds (and bonds)

Leg 3: Real estate exposure

Leg 4: Side hustle

Knock a leg off a dining room table: weight redistributes, and it continues to stand until the damaged area can be reinforced—just like a great financial plan. The legs can even be interchangeable. Maybe you want to substitute cryptocurrency for your real estate holdings; the options are endless. Financial independence requires a multifaceted approach utilizing multiple revenue streams in order to mitigate against the risk of the unknown.

Even after retirement, these rules hold. For instance, one could exchange the W-2 leg with a good insurance policy like a single premium immediate annuity (SPIA) or start taking distributions from a 401(k) account or pension.

> **TERMS**
>
> An **SPIA** is a contract with an insurance company under which you give the company a lump sum of money and the company pays you a set amount every month for the rest of your life.

Don't let the vagaries of diversification scare you. The ultimate destination of each of the three brothers is to build a perpetual money machine to not only provide for you, but also mitigate risk. While the engine for each may be different (front-loading, passive income, or the passion play), all the brothers need to know how to earn, save, and invest to create a diversified financial plan that has at least four legs.

No matter which journey toward financial independence you choose, you are likely to borrow techniques from each of the brothers. Frontloaders may start side hustles to boost income. Passive income warriors will choose a business they are passionate about. And even the most passionate employees can also invest in the stock market.

We should mix techniques, not only to reach financial independence more quickly, but also to spend our time on activities that help strengthen our unique purpose, identity, and connections—to flatten Maslow's pyramid before it's too late.

For those who are most concerned about dying before they enjoy the riches they have accrued, it makes sense to slow this process and allocate less of the savings gap toward building their table and more to spending now on opportunities and experiences. By creating this basic framework (even though less well funded), however, they are building a strong financial base. If they happen to be wrong and live decades longer than they were expecting to, they will still have the fuel to maintain the journey.

And if you are not wrong, and death or disability is coming sooner than you were hoping, it pays to invest in the proper insurance as well as some good financial advice.

THE ROLE OF INSURANCE

Believe it or not, one of the most important decisions in building and maintaining your financial house involves choosing carefully between the insurance options available and deciding how much to become insured for. Most important, for the majority of us insurance is protection against severe or unexpected bad outcomes: loss of life, disability, or significant health care costs. It is not, however, a good form of investment in most cases. I often suggest that, with some rare exceptions, you keep your insurance and your investments separate. The best outcome of insurance is that you paid for a policy that was never used. It is one of those rare instances in which you hope you waste your money.

I wish that could have been the case with my family. Unfortunately, it was not. When my father died in the early 1980s, my mother collected on a policy for $200,000, which compounded enough in the stock market to pay for all her children's college and graduate educations. Although that sounds like a lot of money, it was nowhere near enough. Through a clerical error, a million-dollar policy was promised by my dad's employer but never purchased. How big a difference could a million dollars have made?

Using the 4 percent rule, a million-dollar policy would have assured that my mother could have spent $40,000 a year on our family needs. We would have been considered financially independent by those numbers. My mother could have stopped worrying about her income and retired if she had so chosen. The extra $200,000 would have still been available to pay for our educations.

Instead, my mother was forced to scramble for a job shortly after my father's death. His policy didn't provide enough to shield her from such worries.

As my story shows, insurance can be one of your most important purchases. Let's look at some categories that are worth discussing in a little more depth.

Life insurance. You should have life insurance if you have dependents whom you support. It's that simple. If you have children, a spouse, parents, relatives, or anyone who would be in deep trouble if you no longer provided for them. Notably, single people with no family or dependent relatives probably don't need insurance. Nor do people who are already financially independent. They have assets that create income for them already and don't rely on a job to pay their bills.

The other two decisions, then, are the type and amount of life insurance. Insurance comes in many shapes and derivations, but for our purposes, we are looking at term insurance. The other forms tend to be more investment vehicles and not only are costly but can tie money up for prolonged periods. The amount of insurance is a little more nuanced. Here we are lucky to have already calculated our financial independence net worth number using the 25x method. If you have $40,000 of expenses every year, you should get roughly a million dollars of life insurance ($40,000 x

25). This will allow your family to invest the million dollars immediately and then live off the 4 percent safe withdrawal rate each year. You may also add in other known costs. Maybe you have three children and think that it will take $100,000 to pay for each of them to get a four-year university education. Thus, you can increase the amount to a $1.3 million policy.

TERMS

Term life insurance or **term assurance** is life insurance that provides coverage at a fixed rate of payments for a limited period of time, the relevant term.

Health Insurance. The vast majority of Americans receive health coverage through employers and often pay a fraction of the actual premium. Self-employed individuals, on the other hand, have to obtain insurance on their own and can struggle with high premiums and deductibles. The passage of the Affordable Care Act has been an improvement in some states and has lowered premiums for those who qualify for subsidies. Other options include buying insurance privately through a broker or health care sharing ministry (HCSM).

HCSMs have become popular with the financial independence crowd due to their low costs and broad coverage. They are technically not insurance and are composed of a group of like-minded individuals with similar religious beliefs who come together to share one another's medical burdens.

Long-Term Disability. Everyone who is working should have a long-term disability policy. This is especially important for youngest brothers who rely on a job they are passionate about to produce income to live on. Life insurance will cover your family if you die, but what if you have an accident and don't die but can't work? Where will your income come from then?

There are also several types of disability insurance. Often an employer will provide you with group disability. These policies vary and generally are not as good or inclusive as owning your own policy. They also don't travel with you when you move from job to job.

There are enough nuances about disability insurance to overwhelm our conversation here, but I think that it is best to own your own policy if possible. That policy should be for the maximum amount allowed by the insurer for your income. You can toggle different premium riders such as cost-of-living adjustments (COLAs) that will affect the overall cost of the policy.

I have taken care of many hospice patients for whom disability insurance was pivotal before reaching terminal illness. For instance, Cessaly had been struggling with lupus for decades; she managed to build a successful career in electrical engineering and was the sole financial support for her husband, Kip, and their two children. When she had her first stroke at the age of forty-five, it was clear that she would be unable to perform her usual duties at work. Because Kip would need to stay home to take care of her and the kids, the family would have been bereft without the disability policy provided by Cessaly's employer (her lupus made her ineligible for her own individual policy).

The benefits helped support them for a number of years until a recurrent stroke required hospice care. I remember sitting with Kip at Cessaly's bedside reminiscing about life before she became incapacitated. Even after the first stroke, those disability payments allowed him to be by her side for those precious intervening years at home.

Long-Term Care. Over the years, long-term care insurance has become progressively expensive and thus out of reach for many individuals. It covers expenses incurred if, due to health issues or accidents, you require long-term nursing at home or in a facility, you need equipment, or you have other medical needs. This type of insurance, if you have extra money and can find it at a reasonable cost, should be bought at a young age while the premiums are lowest.

There are many other types and forms of insurance, but for the majority, the ones mentioned here constitute a good primer to getting started with protecting your family and legacy. Remember, insurance generally should not be an investment except for the most sophisticated and wealthy parties.

GETTING THE RIGHT ADVICE

It goes without saying that many of us are "do it yourselfers." We like to navigate the world using our own skills and are loath to pay extra fees for services. But it is also very true that some topics are so specialized that it is worthwhile to include an expert in our team of advisers. There are a few categories of professionals that all mature individuals should have a relationship with.

The goal of these professionals is both to help you more efficiently build your perpetual money machine as well as to identify weakness in your risk management plan. This is especially important for those who worry about dying young and want to leave a stable legacy for those who remain.

The first adviser is an accountant. While many can and do manage their yearly tax returns, if your financial life is going to grow more complex (which is, to some degree, the goal), it will pay handsome returns to get advice from time to time—especially if you are building a business, buying or selling real estate, or taking advantage of some of the more refined tax abatement techniques such as capital gains or loss harvesting.

An estate lawyer is also a good idea. If you are going to draft a will or trust, such a lawyer can be indispensable. Of course, there are online legal resources to do some of this on your own, but a true estate planner can help with the more complex planning issues. The more wealth you accumulate, the more likely you will need a good financially oriented lawyer to help you manage and protect that wealth to pass on to your family.

And now for the most controversial question: Do you need a financial adviser? The answer probably depends on a few issues. If you are comfortable spending a few hours each month learning and reading, and feel confident in your ability to stand strong in the midst of financial turbulence, I think you can save quite a bit of money doing it yourself. The average adviser can charge up to 1 percent of total assets yearly and likely will not boost returns any higher than you will achieve with good old index investing.

On the other hand, advisers are not only about returns. They can help with long-term planning and insurance and be a voice of reason when you are just about to let emotion trick you into a bad decision. It is safe to say that more than 50 percent of you will probably search out an adviser at some point. So if you are going to utilize one, it is important to understand a few key aspects of the relationship.

First, how does the adviser get paid? There are a few different common models. The one I care for least involves an adviser taking a commission for selling you investments or insurance products. Although you are not directly charged for the services, this arrangement leaves the most room for bias. The adviser will be economically incentivized to sell you certain products that may or may not be in your best interest over the long term.

A second and preferable model, in my opinion, involves the adviser being paid a percentage of assets under management (AUM). While this arrangement decreases the likelihood that the adviser will push you into one investment over another, it certainly behooves the adviser to suggest you put all your money into products they offer instead of real estate or building a small business.

The last model, which I think is most beneficial and is affected by the least amount of bias, is the hourly method. You pay the adviser an hourly fee to give you advice. While this arrangement may seem more costly in the short term, I believe it saves money in the form of great advice over the long term.

No matter how your adviser gets paid, you want to make sure that they have reasonable credentials and are acting as a fiduciary. Some certifications to look for include Certified Financial Planner® (CFP), Certified Fund Specialist (CFS), and Chartered Investment Counselor. These will help ensure that your adviser has at least the minimum training and education.

TERMS

Fiduciary financial advisers manage client assets with the clients' best *financial* interests in mind.

Although none of us knows what the future will bring, this should not keep us from getting our financial house in order today. Armed with an understanding of the different paths to financial independence, we can start working on our perpetual money machine. We can weigh what scares us most about money and death and spend now or delay gratification as we see fit.

Insurance and appropriate financial planning can help us ensure that our financial legacy endures whatever tumultuous events overtake us. It did for Cessaly, Kip, and their children. And it can for you, too.

Once you feel like you have a handle on your own finances, it may be time to look toward your loved ones. While you may have come to terms with your own mortality and have started to plan accordingly, often your parents, siblings, or children have not.

Learning how to have these difficult conversations and save yourself and your family from traversing the possible heartache that occurs with poor planning is the subject of the next chapter.

CALCULATING YOUR FINANCIAL INDEPENDENCE NUMBER

1. Clear your schedule for an hour for two to three separate days over the next week. During that time, make sure all electronics are turned to silent, you are well-rested and fed, and you have found a quiet, comfortable place to concentrate.

2. If you have not done so up to this point, choose a method to track your spending. There are several possibilities. Some use a free tracking app such as Mint or Personal Capital. Others prefer to use good old pencil and paper.

3. Look back through credit card and bank statements. What do you spend the most on: food, shelter, transportation? While this may be the perfect time to start practicing those cost-cutting skills, give yourself a moment to look at the numbers without shame or guilt. Remember that larger expenses vary by month. You might have to look at average spending over six to twelve months to get a true feel for the monthly budget.

4. Now, take your monthly budget and multiply first by 12 and then by 25. If you spend $5,000 a month, your calculation will look like this: $5000 x 12 x 25 = $1,500,000.

5. This is your financial independence number at current spending levels. Using the 4 percent rule of thumb, you can safely withdraw $60,000 a year ($1,500,000 x 0.04 = $60,000).

6. Now compare your financial independence number to your current net worth, which you calculated earlier in this chapter. Don't be afraid if they are not even close to each other. You still have a budget to modify, a salary to increase, and years for interest to compound.

7. If your financial independence number feels unattainable, don't be dissuaded just yet. Many underestimate the power of savings, frugality, and compounding. Let the knowledge you have gained from this exercise sink in over a few weeks.

8. After deeper consideration, if these numbers still feel daunting, then the path of the eldest brother may not be for you. Maybe you are a middle? Or a youngest?

CHAPTER 6

IT'S TIME WE TALKED

Being the dutiful son, Matt flew to Chicago from Los Angeles the night prior to our meeting to be well-rested and prepared. His mother's primary care doctor suggested hospice for what could now, finally, be referred to as *end-stage* dementia. Matt felt a surge of gratitude for the unswerving care his father had provided over the last decade. Her papers were in order, and her wishes had been hashed out well before her mental acuity declined. His parents were in good financial shape and could afford the around-the-clock care necessary for Matt's mother to die at home.

I remember assuring Matt that he could return to Los Angeles knowing that his mother was in the best of hands. Little did I know that he would be in Chicago less than a month later trying to avert a crisis that neither he nor I had enough foresight to prevent.

It wasn't his mother's deterioration; we had been planning for that. It was the unexpected bout of COVID that overtook Matt's father and left him unconscious on a ventilator. With horror, Matt realized that not only could he lose both of his parents in a relatively short period of time, but also that he had never been granted his father's financial power of attorney.

If his dad died, Matt would have complete control of his parents' finances as specified in the will and trust set up with their lawyer years ago, before his mother had declined to such an extent. Ironically, Matt automatically acquired the medical power of attorney for both parents by being the closest living relative able to make decisions. But since his father was still alive (though unconscious), Matt had no access to the family finances.

Who was going to pay the hospital bills? Who was going to cover all the extra caregivers they hired to keep his mother comfortable at home?

Our social work team and chaplains volunteered to help Matt navigate the expensive and time-consuming legal path to conservatorship. In a heartbreaking turn of events, Matt's father died before we were able to file the paperwork. Matt's only solace was that now he had access to the funds necessary to support his mother in her last hours of life.

She died just a few days after his father.

TERMS

Conservatorship is the appointment of a guardian by a judge to manage the financial affairs and daily life of another person due to old age or physical or mental limitations.

IF NOT NOW, THEN WHEN?

Stories like Matt's are not uncommon. Even if you have carefully followed the advice of the preceding chapter and your own financial house is in order, you may still have to face difficult decisions regarding your parents, children, or other loved ones. Often the mess is not of your own making, and as in Matt's unfortunate situation, the recognition that something is wrong comes too late.

Believe me, I know that these conversations are anything but easy. They can be complicated and uncomfortable and can result in hurt feelings and frayed nerves. But those difficulties should not stop us from having these conversations. The consequences of not having them are too great, and the solutions are less complicated than most realize.

If you are not going to have this conversation with the people you love now, then when? When they are incapacitated? When they are mourning a physical or emotional loss? When your day in court arrives and you have hired an expensive lawyer to speak for the rights and dignity of a parent who can no longer voice their own wishes? When you are exhausted and unable to express to your children your wishes?

I have had these conversations as a son with my own parents as I have watched them traverse the decades. I have counseled countless sons and daughters as they struggled while a parent courageously faced a terminal illness. And I continue to talk with podcast guests and listeners on *Earn & Invest* as we focus on how to help our family members get their financial lives in order.

Regardless of which hat I'm wearing; I always tend to start the conversation with the same old boring question: "If not now, then when?"

And the answer I receive back is usually the same: "When we figure out how!"

APPROACHING DIFFICULT CONVERSATIONS

Money and death share the dubious distinction of being the most taboo subjects in American culture. We don't like to talk about money. We don't like to talk about death. And we certainly don't want to discuss them together. Yet to avoid finding ourselves in a situation similar to Matt's, and to protect our parents, we're going to have to learn how to destigmatize this conversation. I would love to say there is a one-size-fits-all solution—that there is an easy button waiting to be pushed—but that would be an oversimplification. Just as each of us is an individual with a myriad of complex relationships, the techniques that work for me may fall flat for you. With that being said, there are a few simple approaches to getting started that can introduce this difficult topic.

APPROACH ONE

"Hey, Mom and Dad, I was thinking about meeting with an estate planner to start working on my family's plan in case something were to happen to me. Do you guys have a will or trust set up? What do you think I should do?"

One of the easy ways to broach a difficult subject is to ask for advice, whether you need it or not. This is a great nonconfrontational conversation opener to assess where your parents are at in their estate-planning journey, whether they have even started the process, and how open they are to beginning a discussion with you. While the technique is not absolutely foolproof, your parents' sensing that you need their help will likely make them more receptive to sharing. Furthermore, you may actually learn some helpful tips as they describe what they have created, and you will gain insight into their thought processes.

This technique is especially effective if you are dealing with financially savvy parents who are advanced planners. You can question their decisions under the guise of ironing out your own plan, and discuss with them how their decisions will affect you and the rest of your family members.

APPROACH TWO

"Did I ever introduce you to my friend Matt? The darndest thing happened when his dad got COVID. They realized that no one had been granted access to the family's bank accounts except the mother who was suffering from dementia and the father who was all of a sudden incapacitated on a ventilator. I hope we never face such a situation. What would we do?"

We are profoundly affected by the ordeals and the missteps of our friends and acquaintances. Instead of directly coming out and asking your parents about their financials (which can be awkward and painful), it is often easier to depersonalize the conversation. The horrific situations that have been experienced by others can become a natural segue to a discussion of your own fears and concerns.

The conversation pivots from *what are we going to do with your money* to *how do we protect us all from becoming victims of poor planning*. The idea is to remove the feeling of confrontation and introduce allyship instead.

We are all in this together!

APPROACH THREE

"Hey, Mom and Dad, as I get older, I think a lot about what kind of mark I want to leave on this world. What do you consider your most important legacy for me, my siblings, and all of the grandchildren? How do you want us to remember you when you're gone?"

In its most basic form, estate planning is simply a mechanism of legacy building. How do we want our children, grandchildren, friends, and other family members to remember us? There are two sides to this conversation.

The first is risk abatement. We don't want our family to remember the calamity, poor preparedness, and general disaster that our death left behind. The last thing we want to leave our loved ones is memories of regret and guilt surrounding the small fraction of our lives we spend dying. Hashing out medical and financial powers of attorney, leaving our legal papers in a place where our loved ones can find them, and generally having our wishes known beforehand—steps that would have helped with Matt's near-disastrous situation surrounding his father's death—can go a long way toward allaying this risk.

The second side is defining how our parents will continue to live on in our lives after they are no longer physically present. What objects, stories, and even monies will they leave for us to help celebrate their memory? The old cabin our mom and dad bought that has been used by three generations of the family—will it remain a family keepsake? Will there be funds set aside for the enjoyment of generations to come?

The only way to define what this legacy looks like is to ask them. It's important to clarify that this is not meant to be an exercise in divvying up our parents' wealth to be consumed by family members and others, but more a chance for our parents to leave their mark for years to come.

Notably, it is not enough to use these three techniques to just talk about these important issues. They are meant to be a bridge to actually codify your loved one's legacy. In order to do so, we need to dive into the weeds and discuss what I call the legacy documents.

FINANCIAL LEGACY DOCUMENTS

There is nothing like working in hospice to help remind you of the importance of estate planning. While this is a vast subject to which whole books have been dedicated, some straightforward, simple, and immediate steps will greatly improve our lives and the lives of our parents and loved ones.

You'll note that I have moved away from the words "estate planning" and replaced them with "legacy." These are not documents used to ensure your estate; they are directions meant to strengthen the legacy which your parents (or yourself) leave behind. When we create a series of legal papers that codify these instructions, we are creating legacy documents.

The first, and probably easiest, is reviewing beneficiaries to all our parents' important accounts and insurances. This should be done once a year. Has life changed over the last year? Has there been a divorce, death of a loved one, or a child who is no longer a minor? All of these occurrences may affect whom our parents want to have listed as their beneficiaries. Typically, we are talking about pensions, 401(k)s, IRAs, and life insurance policies.

Jenny never expected to find herself sitting with a hospice chaplain as she watched her forty-year-old husband, Tim, slip away after a massive heart attack. He had appeared to be in perfect health that sunny spring morning when he left the house for a jog. As devastating as the situation was, she felt a moment of solace knowing that the insurance policy he had purchased years earlier would provide for their fledging family.

Imagine the shock she felt when she discovered that the listed beneficiary was an ex-girlfriend. Apparently, Tim had forgotten to update his policy after meeting and marrying Jenny. Fortunately, the accidental beneficiary graciously released the policy to its rightful owner, making an incredibly difficult situation a little bit easier.

You don't want to end up in this situation.

An issue similar to appointing beneficiaries also requires attention: Have your parents assigned a transfer-on-death designation for all other accounts? Often for checking, savings, or brokerage accounts you can specify whom to transfer these accounts to in case of your own death. Why is this important? The bane of all estate planning is something called probate. If you fail to specify a will or an estate plan, you fall under the rules of the state in which you live in. To clarify the distribution of your assets, a process through the court system takes place to rectify and validate all decisions. This process is lengthy and costly, and it drags in lawyers as well as several other parties. You want to avoid probate at all costs!

Many mistakenly believe that a will or testament will avoid probate. This is unfortunately not true. The probate system was actually formed to adjudicate wills. A will is important to make known your wishes on how you would like your money, material objects, and property to be parceled out. Wills can be drafted with the help of an attorney or, if you prefer the do-it-yourself approach, can be researched online. While not always efficient, a will is a great place for your parents to start building their legacy by specifying which of their material objects of importance go to which family members.

TERMS

A **will** or **testament** is a legal document that expresses a person's wishes as to how their property is to be distributed after their death.

If you truly want your loved one's estate to avoid probate, you have to update their beneficiaries regularly, have their transfer-on-death documents in order, and set up a trust. Trusts are also beyond the scope of this book but are worth pursuing with the help of a legal professional after you have covered these other basic aspects of estate planning.

While financial legacy documents are a big part of the planning you need to work on with your parents, if you want to avoid what happened to Matt, you must also address the medicolegal legacy documents at the same time.

MEDICOLEGAL LEGACY DOCUMENTS

There are a host of legal documents that can help ensure that your parents will die with the dignity that they worked to maintain in life. By spending some time discussing and filling out these forms, your parents will leave you with one of the most important possible legacies: knowing you did exactly what they wanted at the end of life. While you will undoubtedly need to talk to your family lawyer and medical doctor to complete these documents, I will provide a brief description of which documents are most essential.

Health Care Power of Attorney. The health care power of attorney (POA) refers to both the document and the person whom your parents (or yourself) can signify to make medical decisions for them if they become incapacitated. Incapacity is usually determined by a medical professional, who will assess the ability of the patient to understand the consequences of decisions and actions surrounding their medical care. It is notable that the POA kicks in only with incapacity. If a person is lucid, they can make their own decisions. In the absence of a formalized document, most states have an automatic succession plan that starts with a legal spouse, then the eldest child, and so on. Although tempting to assign a medical power of attorney and forget it, it is important to realize that this person must both be trustworthy and have an intimate knowledge of what the patient would want done in any given situation. Thus, it pays to have specific as well as philosophical conversations with this person so they can make the right decisions if called upon.

Financial Power of Attorney. The financial power of attorney creates a trusted agent to act on behalf of your parents in financial matters. Your parents do not have to be incapacitated to utilize this agent, and the power of attorney is automatically extinguished upon death (when the financial legacy documents kick in). Unlike the health care POA, there is no automatic succession plan if the correct legal forms are not filed. This was Matt's mistake and could be yours if you are not careful.

Living Will. A living will is a legal written document that specifies what a person would or would not want to have medically done to keep them alive if they cannot speak for themselves. Other preferences such as pain management and organ donation can be spelled out in this document. Whether a person should remain on life support and for how long will be written here. While legally a medical power of attorney should not be able to override the living will, I have certainly seen this happen in real life practice. So, it becomes even more important to have a medical power of attorney who is trusted and aware of the wishes of the person they are supporting.

POLST Form. The Physician Orders for Life-Sustaining Treatment (POLST) form is an attempt to clarify and improve end-of-life care by encouraging providers, patients, and families to discuss critical illness and write a set of specific orders as guidance during a medical crisis. POLST forms vary from state to state, but they usually specify whether someone is to be put on life support or artificial nutrition when they are close to the end of life. This form has largely taken the place of the "do not resuscitate" (DNR) form often used in the past to allow someone to pass away without cardiopulmonary resuscitation (CPR) or other forms of life-prolonging care. Many people, especially those with terminal or chronic illnesses, decide to forgo life support and die in a way they deem to be more quick, peaceful, or natural.

KIDS, IT'S TIME WE TALKED

Up to this point we have focused on the important conversations that children can have with their parents to ensure that their loved ones' financial (and medical) houses are in order. Yet, as our own children age, it behooves us to start these same conversations with them. First, we can follow the advice that we have just given to our parents and start working on our own legacy plan and documents. As my father made me aware, death is not something that happens only to grandparents or those in the later decades of life. If you are old enough to have money, then you are old enough to consider what your legacy will be and to act on that plan.

Second, and just as important, we can start to pass on the financial legacy that we are learning in this book. We can help them sort through the difficulties of navigating the urgency of now and deferring gratification. We can guide them in examining the path of each of the brothers and help them navigate which road to financial independence fits their style.

This is not always easy. My friend J. L. Collins amassed a treasure trove of financial knowledge that he was excited to pass on to his daughter, Jessica. When he approached her while she was in high school, however, she was not ready to absorb or listen to what he had to teach. After several attempts to begin the conversation, he gave up and decided to write a blog to memorialize his thoughts for when she was ready to listen.

His book, *The Simple Path to Wealth*, has now helped educate hundreds of thousands of people on how to get their finances in order and reach financial independence.[26] Years later, Jessica is well on her path to financial stability and has taken her father's advice to heart.

Sometimes, helping your children means realizing their path to financial freedom is much different from yours. During a financial retreat called CampFI in Minnesota, I recently met a father and son who had come to reconcile their significant differences in beliefs regarding money. The father was a physician and a proponent of academia. The son, however, was feeling that university life was not meeting his needs and was much more interested in the entrepreneurial mindset. They both agreed that the reason for financial stability was to give back to their communities and bring about change. The father had suggested the financial independence movement to his son as a viable alternative to the professional path the father himself had taken. They came to the retreat together to learn a new way forward.

The financial legacy we leave our children does not have to be overly complicated. By modeling good and bad behavior, they benefit from our wins and losses. Take the time to communicate with your children and discuss why you have made the decisions you have. Breaking the taboo of talking about money begins one conversation at a time.

FIRE AND ICE

While we have spent much time discussing how to have these difficult conversations with our parents and children, as well as talking about the most important legacy documents, there are a few steps we can take now that will ease the way forward in the sad circumstance of our own untimely death.

Have you completed an ICE binder?

---

26   J. L. Collins, *The Simple Path to Wealth: Your Road Map to Financial Independence and a Rich, Free Life* (Scotts Valley, CA: CreateSpace, June 18, 2016).

I first heard this term while learning about the FIRE movement. Early retirees were creating complex financial plans that might have to span as long as five decades. These plans were riddled with cash, investments, insurance, or even entrepreneurial ventures. Often, one spouse was the holder of all the information, while the other spouse or close family member had no idea about passwords, account balances, or even how the monthly bills were being paid.

Enter the ICE (in case of emergency) binder. The ICE binder contains important financial and social media information for your loved ones in the event of your death or disability. There are several commercially available templates that will allow you to store all your sensitive account and password information in an orderly manner so your loved ones know how to access your financial information and insurance policies.

Over and over again, as a hospice physician, I hear incredible stories about how an ICE binder would have saved a great amount of time and trouble. Jenny and Tim, whom we mentioned earlier in this chapter, probably would have updated all their life insurance policy beneficiaries because they would have been prompted to while filling their binder. Or there is the story of Ernie, who put his valuable coin collection in a nearly impenetrable safe in the garage and then died without telling anyone the combination.

These situations happen all the time and can be quite frustrating for those who are already mourning the loss of a loved one. Wouldn't you want to make their lives easier if you could?

Well, you can.

I began this chapter by asking: *If not now, then when?*

You might think that you are still young. That you have bought yourself a little time by being healthy or getting your own financial house in order. But, as we will discuss in the next chapter, you cannot commoditize time. You cannot buy or sell it.

So what is a person supposed to do?

IF NOT NOW, THEN WHEN?

1. Clear your schedule for an hour for two to three separate days over the next week. During that time, make sure all electronics are turned to silent, you are well-rested and fed, and you have found a quiet, comfortable place to concentrate.

2. You have just had the worst type of premonition. Your life will end in one week. Although this seems strange, you are certain of the truth of this premonition. Take a moment to let the grief engulf you and mourn for all that you and your family are losing.

3. Now think of what you must accomplish over the next few days. Of course, you have to say goodbye to family and friends. Hug and hold your spouse and children one more time. But what else do you need to impart to them?

4. Does your family know how to access all your financial accounts, safes, and social media sites? Does your wife have all the passwords to reset the auto pay for the utility bills? Do they know how to collect your life insurance?

5. Take an empty piece of paper, and list out one by one all the important types of information that your loved ones will need in your absence. Be thorough; include passwords, accounts, anything they will need to manage the financial and other aspects of their lives that you have managed up to this point.

6. Would your family have all the information they would need to know if something happened to you unexpectedly? If you are having trouble making a list of important information, consider buying an ICE (in case of emergency) binder online.

7. Now let's turn the tables. What if it was your spouse or parents who died unexpectedly? Would you know how to access and manage their accounts? If they became critically ill, would you know their wishes or whom they had selected for their powers of attorney?

8. Do you know how to access all their documents?

9. Don't feel bad if this exercise is both physically and emotionally difficult. Most people consider these issues only when the unspeakable happens. How might you benefit from tackling some of these issues now?

PART THREE

THE ONE THING THE DYING WISH THEY HAD MORE OF—TIME

CHAPTER 7

TIME PERCEPTION ARBITRAGE

Although we may not know exactly how many seconds or minutes we have, we are apportioned a limited amount of time on this earth from the day we are born to the day we die. There is no getting around this immutable truth.

TWO STORIES

I want to share two stories of how we experience and conceptualize time. Although we often make the mistake of thinking that time is something we can create or use up—take advantage of or waste—in reality, our options are much more limited. Yet that doesn't mean we should feel completely unable to grab hold of this ephemeral entity. Time doesn't have to be our enemy. We can make it our ally.

LORETTA'S STORY

Loretta had been waiting for ten years. At first, it was only supposed to be a few months until her mother was settled into the new apartment with part-time caregivers. Then, with her mom's unexpected heart attack and resultant weakness, Loretta felt guilty about leaving town. The trip to Paris could wait, as well as the job she had been hoping to take at the craft store. God knows, these were certainly not the ideal circumstances for her to sign up for that new dating app.

By the time hospice care was consulted for her mom's chronic heart failure, Loretta had all but given up on her own needs and interests. Now, at least, she saw an end to the tunnel, even though such thoughts provoked tremendous guilt. It's not that she wanted her mother to die, but it had been almost ten years since Loretta had done anything for herself. She tried to remain cognizant of the fact that, unlike her mother, she herself had time.

Or did she?

One blustery Chicago morning while approaching the nursing home for a visit, Loretta slipped on a patch of ice and broke her ankle. The hospice team helped arrange a room at the nursing home next to her mother's, so that even her ankle rehab wouldn't interrupt the level of support and companionship that had become her preoccupation over the years.

A day later, while trying to stand in her room to fetch a glass of water, Loretta fell to the ground and hit her head. She was dead by the time the ambulance reached the nursing home. Her mother, sleeping quietly in the next room, was completely unaware of what happened.

I will never forget walking into the building to inform my hospice patient that her beloved daughter died the night before from an unexpected accident. The tears flowed down my own eyes as I sat quietly, held her hand, and delivered the horrendous news.

Her mother looked up at me, her face distorted by the devastating effects of age, chronic illness, and now, the unmeasurable pain of acute grief. I will always remember the phrase she whispered into my ear, and how it perfectly captured what we both mourned most in regard to Loretta's premature passing: "Time waits for no one!"

This wasn't the first time I had been stung by this phrase. I remember the exact day when my daughter, Leila, finally grew out of her crib.

THE STORY OF LEILA'S CRIB

We sold it, my wife and I—my daughter's crib. It had been sitting, shoved into the corner, for the past year—since well after Leila got her "big girl bed" and learned how to awaken in the middle of the night and wreak havoc on the household. At first it was just laziness. We kept planning to sell it but never got the chance. Then finally we put up the ad on Craigslist. And the days passed with no interest.

It was a beautiful crib, in pristine condition and stylish. Eventually we dropped the price and relisted it a few times. Nothing in response for days and then, out of nowhere, an email. A young couple in the last few months of their first pregnancy wanted to take a look and would be right over.

They eyed the crib up and down as Leila tried to initiate conversation and my son ran to get his pottery to show the soon-to-be new parents. It took only a minute for them to decide that they would take it. Quickly, I got the tools and started to disassemble what had been Leila's home for the first two years of her life. There was a flurry of activity: unscrewing, lifting, and carrying. Money was exchanged, and we wished the couple well.

As they ambled slowly through our front door carrying the various pieces, it hit me. We had sold Leila's crib! My mind flashed forward to an imagined time in the future. Confined to a nursing home, my addled brain struggling through dementia's cobwebs, I became agitated, and the nursing staff handed me a baby doll. Studies show that it may calm me to care for a pretend child. I would hold the doll thinking that it was Leila and wander aimlessly through the nursing home, searching for a crib to lay her down for her afternoon nap.

But I wouldn't be able to find one, because I had sold it—on Craigslist. And as I stared out the window at the young pregnant woman carefully placing the deconstructed crib in the back of her truck, I felt great regret. Because even before my brain ages and becomes entombed in the plaques and tangles of senility, I couldn't escape the basic fact: no matter how badly I want it to, time waits for no one.

* * *

We are dying from the moment we are born. There is no denying it—no escaping. There are certain unalienable rights that come along with birth, and chief among these is the inevitability of death. This truth challenges our emotional well-being. It creates a mental construct that limits our ability to cope with reality. Try as we might to manipulate the static, there is no changing nature. We can't create or destroy time, and we certainly can't commoditize it.

There is one lever we can pull, however, to change our relationship to this ephemeral concept, and that is *perception*. We perceive time differently at different stages in our life. When we are young, the days and years seem to pass incredibly slowly. We feel as if we have nothing but time. Yet, as we get older, the seasons zoom by. When we are engaged in something difficult, time seems to grind to a halt. When we are having fun, time flies. The saying about bringing up children is especially apt here: *the days are long but the years are short.*

So why is this important?

Since we can't commoditize time, the only form of control we have over our lives is which activities we choose to engage in and how we perceive time passing. Although, at first blush, connecting Loretta's story with Leila's may seem tenuous, taken together they demonstrate the duplicative nature of time. As we watch our children grow, it feels like time passes against our will in a completely uncontrolled manner. Yet, as adults, our time is very much occupied by activities of our choosing. How Loretta "filled" that time was mostly up to her.

In this chapter, I'll share how we can make life feel more valuable and rewarding by understanding the strange science of time hacking: from Parkinson's Law—the old adage that the amount of time that one has to perform a task is the amount of time it will take to complete it—to the Pareto Principle—the idea that 80 percent of our outcomes come from 20 percent of our work.

YOU CAN'T COMMODITIZE TIME

Have you ever listened closely to the verbiage we use when discussing the passage of time? We talk about *buying* and *saving* it. We lament about how we *spend* our time. Our language is transactional—as if we can substitute a very solid and graspable object (money) for something much more fleeting and unwieldy (time). We have difficulty coming to terms with the fact that we can't commoditize time. We are deluding ourselves and paying the price of our own denial.

Within this rigidity, however, there are some choices to be made. Loretta, being the sweet and loving daughter that she was, relegated her hours both emotionally and physically to her mother. Would Loretta have made such choices if she realized she was going to die so soon? Would you?

The point is not to applaud nor criticize Loretta for her choices; taking care of her mother was a noble sacrifice. The tragedy is that Loretta was not cognizant of the fact that she was making such choices in the first place. The vague belief that someday she would get around to her own needs was keeping her blind to the passage of time, and she stopped exerting control over what activities were filling it.

I believe the FIRE community is making the exact opposite mistake. We often feel a much greater sense of control over time than is warranted. We love to say "time is money, and money is time." While this sentiment makes us feel good, our actions confirm that we believe it is utter nonsense. How else do we explain the mad dash to reach financial independence? We might be able to buy our freedom, but we can't turn the hands of the clock back. What then, can we do to combat the inevitable march of time? In my estimation, we are left with the two previously mentioned possibilities with respect to our approach to this slippery phenomenon: either we can better control the activities we choose to participate in while time passes, or we can attempt to modify our perception of time passing. Let's explore both options.

ACTIVITY HACKING: THE EFFICIENT TIME FRONTIER

There is this idea that every hour spent working is an hour that is lost—as if time can somehow be misplaced! Yet nothing could be further from the truth. The hour passes no matter how you choose to amuse yourself.

Sleep an hour—it's gone. Floss your teeth for an hour—disappeared. Sit on the beach in Cancun for an hour...you get the idea.

Ultimately, we are not trading hours or minutes; we are merely living through them. As mentioned in Chapter 2, money is an intermediary. I choose to work as a doctor to accrue this intermediary in order to pay the person who cleans my house or fixes my car. Although I could work less and exchange some hours to go home and do these tasks myself, I prefer listening to hearts and lungs. When given that scenario, I'd rather *spend* (exchange) my time doctoring.

There is no doubt that Loretta used her time to accomplish important things. The comfort and care she gave her mother was priceless. But Loretta also filled a decade with activities that did not cater to her own needs and wishes. We asked earlier whether she would have made the same decisions if she knew she was going to die when she did, but I think this question is an oversimplification. Even if Loretta had far outlived her mother, should she really have spent ten years putting her own needs and wishes on the back burner?

Could she have managed her time more efficiently?

When it comes to investing, we personal finance geeks like to talk about the efficient frontier. This is a part of modern portfolio theory that describes the asset allocation that offers maximal returns with the minimum risk. This makes a lot of sense; we want as high a return as possible with a defined level of risk. We can use the same definition to evaluate our time, but instead of *risk*, we are more accurately talking about *cost*. Now again, when discussing *cost*, I am not referring to the cost of time. Time cannot be bought or sold. I am describing the cost (in both money and emotional reserves) of what activities we choose to pursue during that time.

TERM

Modern portfolio theory, or mean-variance analysis, is a mathematical framework for assembling a portfolio of assets so that the expected return is maximized for a given level of risk.

Our overreaching goal is to perceive time abundance: to feel that we have more time, by far, than we need. While we all agree that this sounds great, many fail to make the daily choices that create such feelings. I believe we can choose to live a life that feels rich in time. We can create space in our routines to slow down, enjoy the urgency of now, and inhabit the moment. It all starts with having the right intentions and then taking actions.

Here are a few actions that can help us feel that we have more time than we felt we did before. As you read these tips, think specifically about how Loretta could have chosen differently.

EARLY TO RISE

Early to bed and early to rise, makes a man healthy, wealthy, and wise. —Ben Franklin

The early morning has gold in its mouth. —Ben Franklin

The early bird gets the worm. —Proverb

How do we feel abundance in a world chocked with scarcity? For me, it starts with my internal alarm clock. I wake up at 4:45 every morning without fail. No matter how hard I try, I just can't stay in bed any longer.

While this early rising might seem rigorous to some, it supercharges my day. I get up, exercise, read, and complete a little work. By seven in the morning, I feel like I have accomplished more than most people do in a whole day. I still have at least fifteen more hours until it's time to sleep again.

Usually, I tackle the most difficult tasks first. I not only have a huge amount of energy, but there also is no one else awake to distract me. There is nothing happening on social media, and I don't receive any urgent phone calls or texts. The easier tasks can be left to later, when I have become more fatigued at the end of the day. Even the best of us becomes a little groggy as the sun sets.

OPTIMIZING

There is also a subtractive quality to time abundance. Not only do we have to spend concerted effort doing what has value for us, we also have to get rid of those activities that consume time (that is, wastes of time) we could be using on more enjoyable or useful undertakings. There are a million time wasters on any given day attempting to suck away our energy.

I found a few ways to combat these over the years: I cancel all useless meetings in the workplace (when I have the authority), I try to cut down and eliminate unnecessary emails, and I often ask colleagues to text me first before calling.

In other words, I have done my best to optimize. I have spent the past decade slowly optimizing my environment. I simply don't want to spend time and energy doing things that can be avoided. Anyone who spends hours emptying their email inbox knows that they can't ever get that time back. My solution is to eliminate the need.

WORK BURSTING

Bursting is the process of accomplishing difficult tasks with intermittent bursts of intense focus. This practice isolates work to highly energetic spurts for brief periods of time. I usually set aside an hour for intense concentration with intermittent breaks of at least another hour filled with less challenging tasks. Not only does this lead to greater concentration and productivity, but it also creates an abundance of downtime in between. Work bursting mixes periods of focused productivity with expansive space to explore less-taxing activities. Bursting works best when done during nontraditional hours—when others are not around to pester you. I like to burst in the early morning. Some like to burst late at night. The point is to create a protected time and space where you can't be distracted.

This is an especially great technique for those who have their own independent businesses and for creatives. If you can control when you perform your work, work bursting may be for you.

OUTSOURCING

The most powerful life hack used to create time abundance is learning how to appropriately outsource. My wife and I use this technique all the time. For instance, we still have a nanny three days a week even though our kids are fourteen and seventeen. They don't need her anymore; we do. We need her to do the dishes, grocery shop, and fold the laundry. We need her to run the countless errands and open the door for the repair person when something goes wrong. It costs some money to continue to employ her, but what better do you have to spend your money on? Is there anything more valuable than time?

In my case at least, I would rather spend more time working (and making money) at something I enjoy to have extra cash to pay someone to do the things around my house that I loathe. I haven't gained or lost time, but I have filled it up with tasks of my choosing at an equivalent cost. I am creating a more efficient time frontier.

I often wonder whether Loretta could have created this same space in her life. Her mother's financials were solid enough to pay for extra care and help—if only she had been willing to spend the money.

By utilizing these techniques, we can create a sense of time abundance. By rising early, optimizing, work bursting, and outsourcing, our schedule can remain open to working, pursuing side projects, enjoying ourselves, and spending time with our families.

Although we can't stop the years from passing, we can do our best to take control of how we spend each day. There are abundant hours in the day, abundant minutes in each hour, and countless seconds.

And for those times when we are stuck doing tasks that we don't enjoy? There is always Parkinson's Law.

PARKINSON'S LAW

As Cyril Parkinson (a British naval historian and author of more than sixty books) noted, we often allow activities we dread to expand and take up greater allotments of time than necessary. While common sense would tell us that we should try to finish these tasks as quickly as possible and then move on and busy ourselves with other things, the reality of how we behave is quite the opposite. As expressed in Parkinson's Law, the amount of time that one has to perform a task is the amount of time it will take to complete the task. There are several interesting corollaries that are worth noting:

- Work complicates to fill the available time.
- If you wait until the last minute, it only takes a minute to do.
- Work contracts to fit in the time we give it.
- Data expands to fill the space available for storage.

TERMS

Parkinson's Law: The concept that the amount of time that one has to perform a task is the amount of time it will take to complete the task.

Although the law is somewhat counterintuitive, I think it is further evidence that you can't commoditize time. Parkinson's Law points to the fact that activities expand and contract, but the time available is constant.

Isn't this exactly what happened to Loretta?

There are several commonsense life modifications we can perform to take advantage of this foible of human nature. The most straightforward is to schedule less time than we think is necessary to perform a given task—or to set no time allotment. We can use work bursting to perform short bursts of concerted high-energy activity with plenty of space for breaks and downtime.

Another good habit is to clearly define what "done" looks like. If we set up specific criteria to signal the end of a task, we are more likely to know when to quit. The key is to know when it's time to stop and realize that perfect can be the enemy of good enough.

Some feel that they are less likely to fall prey to Parkinson's Law if they break big projects into smaller, bite-size pieces with defined and clearly recognizable goals. Boundaries are set to make sure that the scope of work stays within preset guidelines.

And finally, my least favorite approach: some believe in setting up incentives or rewards for finishing early. This tactic has fallen out of favor in my opinion because, as we discussed previously, it relies on external rewards instead of internal motivations.

Whether you choose to use any of these suggestions or not, they are helpful to make sure activities don't unnecessarily expand to fill the rigid boundaries of time. After all, you are likely familiar with the pitfalls of the Pareto Principle.

TERMS

The **Pareto Principle** is the idea that 80 percent of our outcomes usually come from 20 percent of our work.

THE PARETO PRINCIPLE

Known colloquially as the 80/20 rule, the Pareto Principle is often quoted in business and economics. Vilfredo Federico Damaso Pareto was born in 1848 in Italy and became a well-known philosopher and economist. It is said that one day he noticed that 20 percent of the pea plants in his garden produced 80 percent of the healthy pea pods. Expanding on the idea further, he noted that 80 percent of the land in Italy was owned by just 20 percent of the people. His principle thus proclaims that 80 percent of most given outcomes and outputs come from 20 percent of inputs and causes. There are many examples of this principle both inside and outside the financial world. For instance:

- In the US, the top 20 percent of earners paid roughly 80 to 90 percent of federal income taxes in 2000 and 2006.

- The richest 20 percent of the world's population is generating 82.7 percent of the world's income.

- In the US, 20 percent of patients have been found to use 80 percent of health care resources.

Although we generally note the occurrence of this phenomenon in "nature," it is widely believed that the same principle applies to how we achieve results in everyday life. If most of the benefit comes from just a fifth of the work, we may be able to game the situation to continue a high output with much less effort.

And, even more important, often 80 percent is enough—especially if you espouse the idea that perfect is the enemy of good. If we can produce a good enough product with much less effort, we can pivot to other activities to consume our precious time. The key is to realize which 20 percent of your effort is creating the most gains and then stick to that.

We could spend less time on work.

We could be more efficient with chores.

We could create mostly the same value with much less effort.

We could live in a world of time abundance instead of time stress.

TIME PERCEPTION

Learning how to modify your perception of time is a bit trickier. How you do so may be in part dictated by which of the three brothers you identify with. One of the benefits of being the eldest brother and front-loading the sacrifice is that this approach takes advantage of how you perceive time differently during different periods of your life. When you are young, you feel like you have your whole life ahead of you. Time feels infinite, and old age is in the distant future. There is all the time in the world to work and build up enough of your money intermediary. So why not work hard? Why not grind it out? This intermediary will grow and compound over the years. Money is the potential energy in which all those traded work hours are stored. As you age, you'll experience something I like to call time perception arbitrage.

As you get older, your perception of time is much different than it was when you were younger. Time speeds past you faster than you can whip your head around to see it. This time, in a sense, is much more precious and valuable than the time of your youth (which felt endless). If you front-loaded the sacrifice, your store of intermediary (money) can now be used to allow you to only engage in those activities you enjoy. You have enough potential energy to pay for your needs for the rest of your life.

Time perception arbitrage creates a sense of abundance. I may never get those early childhood years back with Leila when I was working so hard; but, being financially independent now, I spend more time with her than ever.

The middle and youngest brothers see the world through a different lens. They are averse to this idea of *wasting* time. While, of course, we understand that is a false construct, they feel that every precious moment should be maximized. Therefore, whether at the beginning of a career or at the end, moments spent in less-than-ideal work conditions are anathema.

In summary, since you can't commoditize time, commoditize the activities you are involved in. Eldest brothers will front-load the sacrifice and use time perception arbitrage to feel as though they have *bought* extra time. Middle and youngest brothers, however, will do the exact opposite. They will find ways to love their jobs now so they can feel that they aren't *losing* any time.

It's all about perception.

TIME ABUNDANCE

The default in the US today is time scarcity, which is shocking given the technology improvements we enjoy compared with just a century ago. From in-house plumbing and electric, to washing machines and dryers, we have to do a lot less manual labor than previous generations did.

A study by the Centers for Disease Control in 2019, analyzing data from the American Time Use Survey, showed that the average American had five hours of free time a day.[27] Five hours! The graph shown in figure 6 breaks down the data based not only by race but also by activity.

---

27   R. Sturm and D. A. Cohen, "Free Time and Physical Activity among Americans 15 Years or Older: Cross-Sectional Analysis of the American Time Use Survey," *Preventing Chronic Disease* 16 (2019): 190017, doi: 10.5888/pcd16.190017.

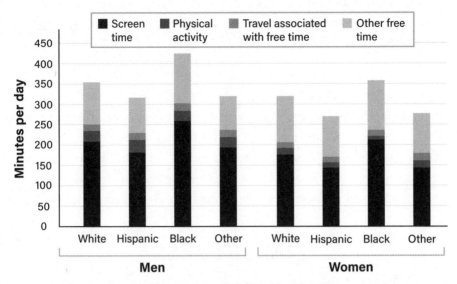

Figure 6. Free time and physical activity

The data also dispels the idea that those who are lower on the income scale and thus may be stuck on the basic needs level of Maslow's pyramid have less free time (see figure 7).

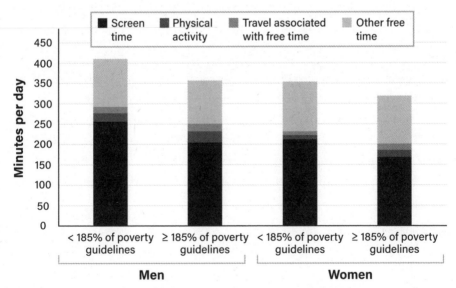

Figure 7. Free time and physical activity by income

A Gallup poll in 2015, however found that, when asked about free time, 48 percent of Americans said they don't feel that they have enough time to do what they want to do.[28] Our perceptions and reality don't seem to match up very well. The clear conclusion that can draw from this data is that we have to change how we perceive time.

Instead of as a commodity, we have to see time for what it is: a space available for us to fill with activities. The space is immobile and unchangeable, and we have absolutely no control over its amount. The activities, however, are completely up to us. And how much we choose to accomplish with those activities is highly dependent on both our mindset and the tactics we have discussed to wrangle Pareto's Principle and Parkinson's Law into an environment of abundance and productivity.

TIME STRESS

There is a cautionary tale about spending too much energy worrying about time. As the studies mentioned in this chapter suggest, our perceptions don't always match reality. This can be positive when we are discussing time perception hacking and using the foibles of our mind to feel as though we are experiencing abundance. I, unfortunately, have suffered most of my life with the dual demons of time scarcity and time stress. My personal story of dealing with time has been one of my biggest mental health issues.

As much as I have tried to change over the years, I am usually under time stress—even when there is little reason. I am constantly aware of every clock in a room and can often be seen glancing up at it. I have spent half my life rushing through activities to make sure that I am in the right place at the right time for the next event. While on the surface this is a good quality, it creates unnecessary stress for myself, my family, and my colleagues.

Why can't I just slow down?

---

28   Frank Newport, "Americas' Perceived Time Crunch No Worse than in Past," Gallup, December 31, 2015, https://news.gallup.com/poll/187982/americans -perceived-time-crunch-no-worse-past.aspx.

It is a question I often ask myself. This tendency can be explained, at least in part, by the great side effects of this mentality. I am superefficient. My awareness of time and my ability to manage a tight schedule have definitely been beneficial throughout my career. These traits have helped in the process of work bursting and have allowed me to manage several disconnected tasks at once.

I tend to show up early to meetings and tasks and usually finish before the allotted time, allowing me to accomplish sometimes double what most people do in an average day. I have found that there are many extra minutes in a twenty-four-hour period. How you use those minutes may be the difference between being extra productive and wasting your time.

The question, however, is whether these benefits are worth the aforementioned dark side. Instead of feeling abundance, I cling to scarcity. And this leads to greater stress and anxiety. Efficiency has its merits, but rushing is rarely good. I bound out of bed every morning and spend the rest of the day running. Does this sound like fun to you? Some days it is fun, but other days it is incredibly tiring.

This is annoying. Not only for me, but those poor people who have to deal with me on a daily basis. While others want to socialize and relax, I am like the Energizer Bunny. I never slow down.

And, worst of all, I hear: "Dad, will you stop rushing me, please?"

I would like to think that this is not a regular complaint from my kids, but I would be lying. Sometimes my time stress bleeds into family events. I can see the look on my wife's face as I zoom out the door while she doesn't even have her jacket on yet. This little foible of mine is often more than just a foible and affects my relationships with the people I love. As much as I try to slow down, I find that my best intentions are like kittens to this lion that afflicts me.

My cautionary tale is to remind us all that altering our time perception can have both positive and negative effects. As I have slowed down on the job and moved further away from the competitive workplace, I have had to learn the art of "wasting" time. This learning has included letting go of the reins and allowing others, such as my wife and kids, to dictate when we leave for family events. I have also used meditation, exercise, and classical music to help me learn how to be more mindful of the present.

I'm a work in progress.

FINAL THOUGHTS ON TIME

The two lessons I have learned from the dying are simple. First, time waits for no one; second, occasionally we just have to slow down. The reason should be intuitive by now: time is not a commodity, although we sometimes choose to see it as one. We try to make time fungible with money. We talk of *saving and spending time*. Some even proclaim that one *is* the other: *time is money*.

Reality, however, is much more sobering. What we perceive as time abundance or scarcity is in actuality our ability to toggle between activities. Although we can't commoditize time, we can budget by choosing the activities that are most meaningful to us and allot sufficient time for them. This is similar, in many ways, to how we budget our resources or excess cash intentionally instead of carelessly frittering our resources away.

We can use certain hacks to manipulate this perception, such as front-loading, early rising, optimizing, work bursting, and outsourcing. We can understand the role of Parkinson's Law and the Pareto Principle and become more efficient at the tasks at hand so we can make room for other activities that we may find more pleasing or a more valuable use of our time. We can also go too far and artificially create a sense of time scarcity and stress, if we are not careful.

The choice is yours!

YOU CAN'T COMMODITIZE TIME: TIME PERCEPTION EXERCISES

1. Clear your schedule for an hour for two to three separate days over the next week. During that time, make sure all electronics are turned to silent, you are well-rested and fed, and you have found a quiet, comfortable place to concentrate.

2. Set your watch or phone timer for one minute. Close your eyes and wait patiently until the minute is up. Now set the timer for a minute again, but this time place yourself in the plank position on the floor and try your best to hold the position for the whole minute. Which minute felt longer?

3. Imagine that you just won the lottery and received $86,400 as one lump sum. You have one day and must spend every single cent. What would you buy? What would you choose not to buy? Would you have money left over at the end of the day? Would you spend frivolously because you had so much?

4. Now recognize that 86,400 is the number of seconds in a day. Does this information change your perception of the exercise above?

5. Take a piece of paper, and divide it into two halves. On the left side, make a list of ten things you did yesterday. On the right side, write down the first five things of great importance to you that come to mind. Now compare both sides of the paper. How much overlap is there? If there is little overlap, why? Was it just an unusual day? Was it representative of most days?

6. Spend thirty minutes writing out your current job description. Be as detailed as you feel you need to. The only rule is that you must not go over a single page. After you finish, do the same thing for a close friend, spouse, or coworker (someone whose job you are familiar with). This time, limit your writing time to five minutes.

7. Compare both descriptions. Is the first description better than the second? Is it five times better? How did your allotment of time change how long it took you to finish the task? Did the extra time result in a better quality description?

8. These exercises are meant to stretch your perception of time and help you understand how you fill your minutes. In the next chapter, we will discuss how we use this resource to make both good and bad (nonmonetary) investments.

CHAPTER 8

INVESTING TIPS FROM A HOSPICE DOCTOR

Although humans often do a lousy job at investing our money, we fail even more completely at investing in ourselves. When I reflect on what my patients have shared with me in their final days, it largely boils down to this conclusion: we need to do a much better job at allocating precious resources for maximum returns.

I'm talking about something more important than cash here. I'm discussing our attention and intentions—what we choose to occupy our minds and hearts with. In her classic book *The Top Five Regrets of the Dying*, Bronnie Ware shares the regrets she most commonly heard during her time in palliative care, which I've found to be consistent with my own experience of what the dying have to teach.[29]

In this chapter, we'll pivot from regrets to investments—those my patients are most proud of and those they grieve. I'll also outline some of the defining characteristics that show the difference between investment and speculation, and I'll highlight key areas where we should always invest frivolously and generously, such as investing in education, your family, and your physical and mental health.

PAUL'S STORY

If cats have nine lives, surely Paul had at least two. There was the one he led for his first thirty years. Lonely and introspective, he struggled with a

---

29   Bronnie Ware, *The Top Five Regrets of the Dying: A Life Transformed by the Dearly Departing* (Carlsbad, CA: Hay House, 2012).

secret that was far too large for his conservative Catholic upbringing. So he closeted his feelings as well his sexual orientation.

His second life began on his thirty-first birthday, when he confessed his heart to his parents. A heated argument ensued, which caught Paul completely by surprise. He left his childhood home in the idyllic Chicago suburbs and never looked back.

A decade later, I stood next to his bed, my body obstructing the stream of light pouring in from the east-facing window of his room. I fidgeted uncomfortably as I asked whether there was something I could do. It was my first day as a volunteer on the hospice unit, and I had never taken care of an AIDS patient before. His partner nodded slowly. They wanted to see the chaplain.

As far as dying people go, Paul had it all: a caring partner, a slew of friends who visited him regularly, and a kind and generous demeanor. Paul rarely complained of physical pain. He could not, however, overcome the internal unrest that snatched the dream of a peaceful death from his frail grasp.

On a sunny October day after receiving a call from the chaplain, his family rushed the short distance from the suburbs to the city hospital. By the time they entered his room, he was unconscious.

The chaplain asked that they hold hands to say a prayer. And there stood Paul's loved ones: his father holding the hand of Paul's partner; Paul's mother and sister standing among his friends. Paul's eyes opened briefly before he took his last breath. As he looked up, a faint smile formed at the corner of his lips; he could die now.

CHANGE IS FOR THE LIVING, NOT THE DYING

Anyone can change; it is never too late. In my years working in hospice, I have seen many last-minute reconciliations like the one between Paul and his family. The deus ex machina, or grand plot twist, is not only an overused storyline—it happens in real life. Yet, relying on such antics is more a symptom of poor planning than a true solution.

Wouldn't Paul and his family have been much happier and healthier if they had reconciled years earlier? How much time could they have spent together? There is both beauty and tragedy in the telling of Paul's story.

We need to learn how to change now, before it's too late, before we are on our deathbeds. The regrets of the dying rarely focus on money and career, and yet we would be remiss in not recognizing their role as enablers. Building your own path to financial independence removes one roadblock. But like Maslow's flattened pyramid, we must learn how to climb not stepwise, but simultaneously. We must work on our wealth and our self-actualization in tandem—long before we find ourselves in Paul's situation.

In figure 8, I have relisted Bronnie Ware's five regrets of the dying, which we discussed in Chapter 3. After many years of hospice work, I think not in terms of regrets, but rather in terms of investments. What investments are my patients most proud of, and for which do they feel remorse? How can we, the young and healthy, learn from this knowledge?

TOP FIVE REGRETS OF THE DYING

1. I wish I'd had the courage to live a life true to myself, not the life others expected of me.
2. I wish I hadn't worked so hard.
3. I wish I'd had the courage to express my feelings.
4. I wish I had stayed in touch with my friends.
5. I wish I had let myself be happier.

Figure 8. What the dying regret

THE POWER OF RECONCILIATION

Often the dying wish they had invested more in the power of reconciliation. I have been confided in dozens of times as a patient lay near death. The story of Paul and his family is but one example. Humans hurt one another; it is in our DNA. The only force greater than our ability to inflict pain is our capacity to love and forgive. This dance is as old as human life itself. The dying whisper their wisdom as they struggle to repair broken relationships and hurt feelings. They urge us to invest in mending fences long before the end of life is near.

And reconciliation is not just about people who have hurt us, but also about those we have misplaced along the way. There doesn't have to be bad blood for us to lose touch with someone who was once important to us. Whether a former lover, friend, or family member, we crave not only a sense of closure, but also, possibly, a new beginning.

Why wait until you are on your deathbed to try to fix what has become disjointed and frayed? Why not take the difficult step of reaching out now, when time and health are on your side? Can you imagine how wonderful it would be to reconnect with these important people in your life and have years to explore the relationship? Years to forgive and be forgiven? Decades to start anew?

It would be downright magical.

THE COURAGE TO FAIL

Failing—or more correctly, not failing enough—is a major regret of the dying. I seldom witness a person complaining on their deathbed that they tried their best and yet didn't succeed. We accept the inevitability of occasionally failing after an honest effort has been made. Failure is an incredibly common part of our lives: we sometimes fail as parents, as employees, and even as human beings.

Ernesto relished vividly, on his deathbed, the memory of trekking up Mount Everest after years of training. He remembered the wind in his face and the cool crisp air. He didn't, however, waste much time thinking about the fact that an unexpected snowstorm ended his venture prematurely. He made it nowhere near the summit—a fact that burned a lot less over the years. He felt a sense of peace knowing that he had done his best.

We need to have the courage to invest in failing bravely, without fear or remorse. We must overcome the inertia to do nothing when doing something is what our heart really desires. Living in harmony with your true purpose, identity, and connections is not easy. There are always hurdles and roadblocks around every turn. And, what is even more terrifying, we may not succeed.

Ernesto never reached his ultimate goal.

This fear of not succeeding is often enough to stop us dead in our tracks or, even worse, motivate us to put off today what we can do tomorrow. As the tomorrows pass, the likelihood that we will develop the courage diminishes.

It takes only a short time working with the dying to realize that none of those tomorrows are guaranteed. How many times do I have to hear the same regretful laments?

- I wish I had the courage to do...
- I wish I had the strength to say...
- If only I was brave enough to try...

No one can tell you how to complete these statements. But I do know that it's worth the time and heartache to start asking those questions now, before we are measuring our time on this earth in days or months. You will never regret the shortcomings you become aware of through valiant effort—only the ones you never fought for.

That is not to say that all unfinished plans are bad or even cause for regret. Those who live an active life full of wonder and investigation may breathe their last breath with a full bucket list; even in our last days, we can still be engaged in *the climb*.

My personal homage to the courage to fail is the writing of this book. For many years, I pulled out almost every excuse not to start: *What if I don't succeed? What if I fall on my face? What if no one reads it?* My years tending to the dying have forced me to ask an even more important question: *What if I die before I give myself the chance to try?*

As Theodore Roosevelt opined in his famous 1910 speech, It is better to be "the man in the arena" or "doer of deeds" than the critic on the sideline.[30]

Human beings have become expert self-critics—and we pay dearly for this expertise.

LIVING IN THE MOMENT

Life passes by quickly—sad but true. The days may seem long, but the years are short. We spend many of those days concerning ourselves with long-term goals. Delayed gratification builds a strong and stable future. Being overly goal-centered, however, can detract from learning how to enjoy the here and now.

Our default is to wander the earth preoccupied. We allow our minds to continuously spin, contemplating our next goal, accomplishment, or task laid out in front of us. The unintended consequence, unfortunately, is that we fail to invest in the urgency or the joy of now.

How many Sunday evenings have been ruined by the prospect of a Monday morning at work? How many vacations have prematurely ended in your mind when you think about the hassle of returning—even when you still have a few more days left?

The dying rarely savor the memory of Monday mornings or the plane trip home from vacation. They cherish the moments in between with family and friends—the rush of cool air and the warmth of the blazing sun as they stood in the sand on a tropical beach.

We have become imprisoned by our thoughts and machinations, and have forgotten how to enjoy the experience; we have forgotten how to live in the moment. The solution is simple yet effective. Like Ernesto, we must learn how to revel in the climb and let go of the destination as our ulti-

---

30   Theodore Roosevelt, *The Man in the Arena: The Selected Writings of Theodore Roosevelt; A Reader*, ed. Brian M. Thomsen (New York: Forge, 2003).

mate goal. While reaching the summit of Mount Everest was not in the cards, Ernesto recognized the beauty of each step as he took it. It was just him and the mountain, the cool crisp air, and the feeling of his calf muscles as he pushed forward into the unknown.

CHASING FALSE GODS

The dying often feel grief over the all-too-human penchant for investing in and chasing false gods. I'm not talking religion here. Working with those who are close to death has made me think a great deal about whom and what we choose to deify. What and whom do we worship? At the end of life, regrets abound surrounding aspects of life that we thought were important but ultimately realized were not—the false gods.

Money and career are at the top of the list. I have never—never—heard anyone say they wished they worked harder at their job or accumulated more wealth as they lie on their deathbed. I have never heard someone regret that they should have spent more nights and weekends in the office. In fact, the exact opposite is mostly true. Often, I hear people complain that they shouldn't have worked so hard. They regret not investing more time with families, enjoying experiences, or living in the here and now.

Materialism is another false god. No matter how much we accumulate, it is of little comfort when terminally ill. Your stuff can't love you back. When I do see patients derive happiness through material possessions, it is often more an issue of sentimental value. We hold on to the stuff that remind us of the people we love or of our own personal accomplishments that are meaningful.

Consider the difference between Connor Sr., the patriarch from Chapter 1 who died in the hospital wing he paid for, and Anne, the poetess from Chapter 2. Connor had all the wealth in the world but died feeling utterly alone in a sterile hospital room. Anne, on the other hand, passed quietly in her sleep surrounded by her papers, books, and poetry.

Which would you prefer for yourself?

Power is another intoxicant we tend to invest in while healthy that falls swiftly away when death is lurking around the corner. It gives us quite a shock to realize that no matter how much importance we have accumulated, no matter how many titles we hold, the world will go on without us when the time comes.

Take a moment now to ponder your own insignificance. Do you find it depressing or freeing? Your response will help you understand the role of power in your sense of self-worth.

And finally, we must stop investing in the incredibly destructive false god of perfection. I have said before that perfect is the enemy of good. It can also be the enemy of sanity. We spend countless hours or even years being unsatisfied with aspects of our lives that are, in truth, better than average—whether it is our careers, our looks, or even our intellect.

I'm not saying that self-improvement is a bad thing. There is a limit, however, in how striving for perfection improves our lives. When taken too far, we cause a great deal of mental suffering and deprivation to boost ourselves those last few percentage points for minimal gain. We long for perfection to prove that we *went all the way* or *gave it our all*.

The danger is that we develop a narrow focus, ignore those we love, and neglect other important life goals.

Perfection is rarely worth it.

And neither, by the way, is speculation.

THE DIFFERENCE BETWEEN INVESTMENT AND SPECULATION

Whether a young adult newly facing the world or an elderly person with a terminal illness, knowing the difference between investment and speculation will ultimately have a profound effect on your sense of well-being in all stages of life. In the real world, both high-income earners and novices mistake these two principles.

While there is definitely room for speculation in almost any human venture (economic or otherwise), investment should be where the majority of our resources are stored and allowed to grow. So, what are some of the defining characteristics that demonstrate the difference between investment and speculation?

TIME VERSUS LUCK

Investments grow over time. Any investment—a fund, stock, bond, business, skill, passion, or relationship—has measurable value. That value is expected to increase over the years to be greater than it was previously. The value can take many forms—anything from a dividend payment to a new skill. Work is often involved, as exemplified by building a business. But work may be unnecessary, as in holding a mutual fund. Either way, the passage of time and compounding do a majority of, if not all, the heavy lifting.

Speculation relies mostly on luck. Time may or may not be beneficial. Luck may take many forms. An asset can be purchased below market value and sold immediately for a gain. In another scenario, a product can be bought at market value but then artfully sold for an inflated price. Finally, after a product is acquired, a skill learned, or a relationship formed, the market can change, making these assets more valuable.

Speculators are risk-takers by nature.

RISK MANAGERS VERSUS RISK-TAKERS

Investors are risk managers. They mitigate risk by hedging their bets. They are leery of expending money, time, or energy until they are assured of a successful outcome. They invest in stocks and businesses as well as skills and relationships. They perform due diligence and they monitor their efforts carefully.

Speculators, on the other hand, are risk-takers. They make decisions based on intuition, a hot tip, or their own ability to manipulate the situation.

Examples abound.

Putting money in an S&P 500 index fund (a fund holding five hundred large US companies) is an investment. Based on the endurance of the US economy, past performance, and the adjustable nature of the index, it is likely that over extended periods of time the value will multiply.

Taking your brother-in-law's suggestion to buy stock in a start-up company with no history of profits is speculation (and quite risky at that)—especially if you have no knowledge of the industry, the company has yet to prove itself, and there is no written business plan.

Putting time and effort into getting to know your spouse's best friend is an investment. The benefits will likely compound over the long term and create a deeper bond with your spouse.

On the other hand, spending time and energy befriending your spouse's work acquaintance whom you see once a year at your spouse's company Christmas party is speculation. The relationship could potentially pay off in the end, but it is unlikely that it will.

It is notable that even speculative ventures can and do sometimes produce large profits. But they more often produce nothing. The difference is luck.

Based on which of these examples you relate to most, are you a risk-taker or a risk manager?

EFFICIENCY VERSUS INEFFICIENCY

For the most part, investors rarely try to exploit market inefficiencies. Investors pay fair value for an asset they feel is going to grow, and then they allow time to do the work for them.

> **TERMS**
>
> The efficient-market hypothesis, in financial economics, states that asset prices reflect all available information.

A perfect example is investing in a career. You might attend a program that provides a high likelihood of long-lasting employment, like computer programming. There is a strong chance these jobs will be abundant far into the future, but you would be silly to place all your eggs in the newest, hottest coding language—it may die out or be replaced in the near term.

Speculators love market inefficiency. They want to buy low and sell high. Or buy high and sell higher. They want to jump into the latest fad. The innate value of an asset or a skill, or its growth projections, is not nearly as important as how quickly they can take advantage of a mismatch between price and value, supply and demand.

In conclusion, investors are risk managers who use their knowledge, risk mitigation strategies, and time to profit from an efficient market. Speculators are risk-takers who pray for market inefficiencies and hope luck will go their way.

How does this play out in our lives? How can we use our knowledge of investment and speculation to help us do better today? What should we be investing in? Here's my experience as a hospice doctor.

INVESTING TIPS FROM A HOSPICE DOCTOR

I used to have a patient who was an undertaker. We had many conversations about philosophy and practicality, and it didn't take long for me to realize that one must gain profound insights from being engaged in such a unique business. As I was often fond of saying, *when the undertaker speaks, you should really listen.* Those of us who have made death and dying our business may seem unlikely investment advisers, but because both the undertaker and myself have spent extensive time in close proximity to mortality, we've been given unique insight into what's really worth investing in. What good investing tips could someone in my line of business have gleaned from dealing with death and dying? Believe it or not, a few quickly come to mind. These tips were not learned by accompanying the wealthy through this difficult journey—although the wealthy have much to teach. These tips were not siphoned off of the personal books of those who had little interest left in hiding their secret ingredients to success. These are simple, straightforward bits of knowledge gained from walking down this lonely path with those reluctant to be making the journey.

And believe it or not, most of what I learned about investing has nothing to do with money.

INVEST IN YOURSELF

Personal investment comes in many forms. Chief among these is self-forgiveness. Remorse is common in humans of all stripes—living and dying—and its effects can be devastating. The specifics may vary: an action taken or not taken, a relationship salvaged or destroyed, or an object bought or sold. The human capacity to blame oneself is unlimited. We spend endless amounts of time feeling bad about things we wish we had done better. While self-blame serves the purpose of introspection and improving future outcomes, it often leaves a path of destruction it its wake. It is hard to look forward when you are constantly looking back. The key appears to be changing what we can change and forgiving ourselves for the rest.

Losing his job was the least of Gerald's regrets. Decades before being diagnosed with cirrhosis (chronic liver disease), his exit from corporate America set off a series of events that ended in alcoholism. His marriage fell apart, and he quickly became estranged from his ex-wife and his daughter, Sandy. While sobriety and eventual employment were recoverable, the damage he had done to his body was not. Neither was the estrangement with Sandy. A large part of the life review process was spent with the social worker exploring his feelings surrounding the loss of his daughter. Gerald eventually was able to find a modicum of peace and forgive himself. He also realized that if this self-forgiveness had been granted earlier, he might have been able to quit alcohol long before his liver became so damaged.

What have you been unwilling to forgive yourself for? What damage is this unwillingness inflicting?

Another common way we invest in ourselves is by slowing down. Often, we have big audacious goals and want to reach them immediately. Yet—

as in the story of the turtle and the hare—slow incremental gain is what helps us win the race. If we can make progress toward a major goal by just 1 percent per month, we will have phenomenal annual returns over the long run. This principle applies to a skill, a relationship, or just about anything we strive toward. We must not allow our limiting beliefs to hold us back.

> **TERMS**
>
> A **limiting belief** is something you believe to be true about yourself, about others, or about the world that limits you in some way.

We also need to invest in experiences. Experience compounds over time, just as our monetary assets do. As we learn and grow, we hone skills that make us better employees as well as people. Ask anyone who has risen through the ranks to become CEO of a company. Just like Ben Franklin's compounding investments, growth in the workplace is anything but linear; it grows exponentially.

And if we are going to talk about investing in ourselves, we would be remiss if we didn't mention education.

INVEST IN EDUCATION

While there is no question that I have benefited from an expensive four-year college education, there are so many different ways to educate yourself nowadays—read, discuss, take online courses, debate until your face is blue and you walk out of the room disgusted. The world is full of teachers, great and small. Knowledge is the emergency fund in which you shield your happiness. When all other resources are exhausted, your knowledge will help you secure a job, build a shelter, or make the right decisions at the most critical moments. Do not skimp on self-improvement, and don't be afraid to pay for it. The money you spend on education will compound in the form of knowledge and skills.

Say yes—even when you don't want to. Open yourself to other people's requests, and jump into an activity that feels foreign or uncomfortable.

The only way to gain knowledge or discover new passions is to be willing to explore. Not only will you be exposed to exciting opportunities, but you will also build stronger relationships with those to whom you say yes. Always have your bags packed.

Don't be afraid to learn new things. I am continuously surprised by how resistant the average person is to learn about basic finance. Most experts suggest that a few hours of reading each month will make you totally financially competent. Yet the preconceived notion that the subject is too difficult scares many away; don't let it.

I have watched countless patients die with a book on their nightstand or an unfinished argument circling their brain. This is not sad or trivial. Even those who are dying wake up every morning with a plan for how they will spend each day. Make sure you allow room for acquiring new knowledge. Inquisitive people tend to die as they live: happy and full of questions.

INVEST IN OTHER PEOPLE

The one measure of a person (rich or poor, happy or sad) is in the people whom the person leaves behind. I can think of no greater indicator of success. I know instantly when I walk into the room of a dying patient whether they have invested in other people. They are surrounded by pictures, letters, cards, and friends.

In fact, I usually know who the successful investors are before I even reach the hospital room. There are people walking in and out; noise and laughter peal through the otherwise somber hallways. Smiles and tears celebrate the bittersweet confluence of life and death.

If you invest in people, the compound interest will multiply into a lifetime of love and happiness. Long after you are gone, your essence will survive in the smile on the lips of those who shared in your asset allocation.

It took me years to understand this tip. I stumbled about as a doctor looking to find my people in the midst of a community that didn't fit me. It was only after I discovered writing and podcasting in the personal finance realm that I was able to connect with people who understand me.

These connections have made all the difference; they have given me the courage to redefine my identity and purpose.

INVEST IN CHILDREN

Invest not only your money, but your time and love. Invest in children. Help build the blocks of their adulthood and happiness. Sprinkle them with your knowledge, humility, and kindness. Lead them with your virtuous example. In you, they will find the role model of success and freedom. Teach them about finances so they can understand what money can and can't do for them in attainment of their life goals. Leave them with a good example of what living looks like.

Investing in your children will produce a lifetime of dividends. They will be the shoulder to lean on and the undertaker of your vast life dreams. Your time on this earth is short, but your progeny will carry on your spark. Like a ripple in a vast ocean, your effect will be carried with them through the generations. You will live on in the hearts and minds of those who come after you.

Every time a colleague accidentally calls me by my father's name, while rounding at the hospital, is proof of how we live on in our children. His legacy shaped my career and passions even decades after he has passed. He is remembered.

I will never be able to repay my parents for what they have willingly surrendered to me. Instead, I will pay it forward to my own children. I will invest in them in much the same way as my parents have invested in me, and, thus, our goodness will continue on through the generations.

INVEST IN PHYSICAL AND MENTAL HEALTH

Your body and mind are interconnected. They form the framework you build upon. There is no financial well-being without mental and physical well-being. As this book demonstrates, managing your money and future take forethought and conscientious decision-making. You can't do this properly if you yourself are unwell.

Invest in mental health by taking the time and energy to recover. Learn how to slow your mind and relax with activities such as meditation, exercise, and listening to classical music. Don't be afraid to ask for help from family, friends, or mental health professionals. Psychological counseling is not only common but also incredibly helpful. Getting a professional's outside perspective can make a huge difference in quieting those internal voices that disrupt your peace and calm.

Physical health also plays an important role. Not only may it prolong the time to the end of life, but the emotional benefits are also enduring. We generally feel stronger both physically and emotionally when we are taking positive steps to take care of ourselves. This does not mean that we all have to become marathon runners. As I said before, perfect can be the enemy of good enough.

Try to get at least thirty minutes of physical activity a day. Start with something easy like walking. Find an activity that fulfills your physical needs without being loathsome or burdensome. If you hate doing it, the habit will not last.

While I do not feel strongly about alcohol or drugs, anything above recreational use often limits our health as well as our ability to see our goals clearly. If you are wondering whether it's a problem, then it probably is. Most of the highs these substances give us are artificial and short-lived.

INVEST IN THE MARKET

Even a collection of investing tips from a hospice doctor would be remiss without the basics. This is a personal finance book, after all. So, don't forget to invest in the stock market:

- Earn more than you spend.
- Save as much as you can each year (20 to 50 percent).
- Buy broad-based low-cost mutual funds.
- Max out retirement savings first, and then open a taxable brokerage account.
- Hire a financial adviser only to advise—not to invest for you.

My hope is that this book gives you the intellectual, tactical, and practical knowledge to get the money right so that you can invest more heavily in the other things I've discussed. I do not want to minimize the importance of understanding the financial basics, but I do want to remind you that they are necessary but not sufficient.

These are my investing tips from a hospice doctor. As you can see, only the last section deals with money. The reason, of course, is that finances are the easy part. How you invest the rest of your time and energy is likely to determine your perspective in those waning days when you deal with a doctor like me. Don't waste your life and regret.

Start investing now! Before it's too late. The stronger the foundation you create, the better you'll be able to deal with the unexpected. Because if you haven't figured it out yet, that is the point of investing in the first place. No matter how much we protect ourselves, there is no way to predict the future. We use the term "black swan events" to discuss truly rare and unexpected events that have a profound impact on our life and finances. More common, however, are white swan events. They are often impossible to time, but we will experience a few of them, and they are likely to test how well we have truly invested.

My family found this out when my father died.

TERMS

A **white swan event** is a common but difficult-to-time event that has significant financial impacts on a person. Some examples include divorce, family death, or illness.

IRONY AND LIFE INSURANCE

I didn't pay for college or medical school; my mom did. In fact, I started my adult life with zero debt. Unlike for some, the reason wasn't that I won scholarships, had a mentor, or created a stupendous hack to break the system. I didn't even work my way through (I've always worked but never enough to pay off such debts). Nope. My mom paid for it—every single cent.

But it wasn't free.

My dad died when I was seven years old. He had a brain aneurysm and collapsed while rounding at the hospital. A life's worth of hopes and dreams were gone. My mom, myself, and two brothers were left behind.

My mother, the accountant, took the $200,000 of life insurance and invested it in the early 1980s. And it grew, and grew, and grew—compounding through a wild ride in the stock market.

A single life insurance policy sent three children through college, two through graduate school, and one through medical school. The last of the money was distributed to each of us in the form of $15,000-dollar checks in the early 2000s.

Ironically, when it came time to renew my own term life insurance policy recently, I couldn't help but think of my dad. His legacy had driven me to become a doctor, and his insurance had paved the way.

After buying my own life insurance policy years ago, I have since become financially independent and can self-insure. If my wife and I can stop working at any time, we certainly no longer need to insure our lives. Our children won't need more than we already have.

So it was with a feeling of great heaviness and irony that I canceled my policy—a policy similar to the one my father had lovingly left us. A policy that I no longer had any use for.

INVESTING HELPS PREPARE FOR THE UNEXPECTED

I decided to tell the story of my dad and life insurance to remind us that investing helps prepare for the unexpected. We do not know what the future holds other than the certainty that someday we are going to die. This is an immutable fact. As I've said before, we are dying from the day we are born; the when, where, and how remain a mystery.

The dying have an important story to tell. Through their eyes we are able to see what really matters. They judge their successes and regrets by how well they invested their time, talents, relationships, skills, love—and, yes, even their money.

They were only able to read the tea leaves to a certain extent. They were unaware of whether joy or tragedy was lurking around the corner. They were clueless about which black swan or white swan events awaited them. Yet the lesson to be learned couldn't be clearer; prepare yourself through wise investment.

My father had an insurance policy that paid out when he died unexpectedly at forty years old. He and my mom were prepared for the worst—thank God. Their monetary investments hadn't had enough time to grow and protect us, but their insurance could.

I canceled my life insurance policy at the age of forty-six when my financial investments exceeded my family's needs. Should I unfortunately follow in my father's footsteps, my family will be taken care of even without my life insurance.

There are no insurance policies, however, for the nonmonetary types of investments that I have mentioned in this chapter. There is no protection plan, no deus ex machina that is going to save the day, no easy button.

Your investing plan has to start immediately—before you are dying and the end is so clearly in sight. Building a life of meaning, purpose, and connections takes time and compounding. Investing in yourself takes energy, and investing in education requires work. Building relationships with your children and community will be a mental and physical strain. Taking care of your mind and body will be taxing. Learning about personal finance and building financial security will consume hours that you might rather have spent on something else.

And it is all so very, very worth it. Be as prepared for life as you would be for death.

Invest in yourself wisely.

THE INTEREST OF TIME: NONMONETARY INVESTMENT INVENTORY

1. Clear your schedule for an hour for two to three separate days over the next week. During that time, make sure all electronics are turned to silent, you are well-rested and fed, and you have found a quiet, comfortable place to concentrate.

2. Take a sheet of paper, and separate it lengthwise into three separate columns. Number each from 1 to 10.

3. For your first list, write down all the education you have received up to this time. You can start with high school, university, or college. Add in any graduate programs, online courses, on-site work trainings, or self-study projects. Be generous here—no need to have received a formal degree or certificate. It's OK, especially for this section, if you don't have ten full entries.

4. For your second list, write down all your skills. These can range from professional expertise to innate talents to self-taught abilities. Don't forget all that you have learned through social media. Are you a content creator? What about hobbies? Again, give yourself credit. What do people always tell you that you are good at?

5. Finally, in the last column write down key relationships. This includes family, friends, work associates, and even acquaintances. List the ten people who have a big influence on your life. This is your community.

6. Now peruse your three lists together; this is the sum total of your nonmonetary investments. What you have created is an inventory of your nonfinancial wealth. Often, we get so caught up in our net worth calculation that we forget about our nonmonetary assets.

7. If you take your inventory of nonfinancial wealth and add it to your net worth calculation, you now have a true listing of all your resources. Are these enough to allow you to utilize most of your time pursuing your true purpose, identity, and connections? If so—welcome to financial independence!

CONCLUSION: THE D WORD

I remember when my daughter as a young child began to use the "D word."

When I die, people will walk on me?

Even at the age of four, she knew that the dead are buried in the ground. More questions followed rapidly. She thought that if a grandparent didn't show up to pick up a classmate from school one day, the grandparent must have died. She had the same thought if someone went on vacation for a week.

Her statements were unsophisticated but shockingly honest. Unfettered by the complexities of the adult mind, she was free to explore unencumbered. There was no guilt or embarrassment in her voice. Our conversations lacked the fear and angst that so often cloud this kind of discussion among grown-ups. She was curious.

Was I dead before you had me?

In some ways, my daughter's fascination with death has not evolved as she has grown older. She has lost the innocence as she has moved past the details and begins to contemplate deeper meaning.

What happens to our soul?

The pang of love that shatters our hearts—does it just disappear?

And I tell her that I don't know. I have helplessly watched life slip away countless times, but I am no closer to the answers to these questions. I have both battled death as the enemy and humbly welcomed its mercy. I have traveled its paths and attempted to veer away at every turn. I no longer see death as friend or foe, but more as a quiet presence waiting patiently in the wings.

Like my daughter, we are all just children. Bobbing and floating in the vast ocean of life, our minds turn, yet we have no control over the direction of the tide. My daughter's voice pulls me back to the little bed in her quiet room so many years ago. "Daddy, what does it feel like to die?"

I drew her in close and held her tightly. "My sweet child, I'm still trying to figure out what it feels like to live."

* * *

We are not very skilled at discussing the D word. Take it from someone who has now spent his career learning how to help people cope not only with the physical symptoms but also with the emotional baggage that comes along with death. As we do with the topic of money, we avoid discussions about death until we absolutely must have them—until we are either diagnosed with a terminal illness or forced into a financial corner. We suffer in silence because these subjects are taboo; we fear discussion will either hasten their arrival or adversely affect the outcome.

Fear is the driver that causes us to manage both so poorly. Yet as my discussion with my daughter so concisely points out, if we want to learn how to die better, we have to learn how to live. And if we want to learn how to live better, we have to tackle the difficult questions surrounding what money means in our lives and how we define "enough."

The dying, saddled with a terminal illness and a limited amount of time, often are forced to review their lives and either make quick changes or come to terms with all that has occurred, good and bad. When things go well, dreams are met, and relationships are repaired, we celebrate the deus ex machina (the magic of a plot twist at the end that brings resolution).

I wrote this book to relieve you of the necessity of the dramatic plot twist. What if we can learn now from the dying and get our affairs in order much sooner? Maslow might have called this concept self-actualization. Happiness researchers prefer "emotional well-being" and "life evaluation."

I envision using our lives to pursue our own unique purpose, identity, and connections. The concepts all have similar meanings.

To get our affairs in order when we still have time, we need to disentangle money from happiness and flatten Maslow's pyramid. I believe that we can aspire to achieve all levels simultaneously. Waiting for financial security unnecessarily delays some of the deepest and most important work we do as human beings. The dying can help us with this difficult process. They can enlighten us. They can show us how to change before it's too late.

In the first section of this book, we focused on what financial experts get wrong about life and death. We illustrate through Connor's and Charlie's stories that often our conception of "enough" is skewed. We should strive for economic well-being as well as self-actualization simultaneously. We must also recognize the dangers of the hedonic treadmill and overdrive. Often, when it comes to financial issues, our wheels are spinning, but we are not going anywhere.

Money has the capacity to bring happiness only to a limited extent. There are countless studies that show that after a certain level of income or wealth, our sense of well-being no longer increases. That doesn't mean that we should abandon all attempts at fiscal responsibility but instead see it as one piece of an interconnected puzzle. Our financial goals are not an end point but rather a lever that help us strive toward *the climb*— consistent progress toward a meaningful goal.

Often our true concept of "enough" becomes clear only when we participate in a life review process similar to what occurs in hospice. But why should we wait until we are ensconced in our deathbeds? There is no time like the present.

The life review process helps us see through the money mirage and other false economic goals. We need to completely change the way we define such terms as "work," "employment," and "retirement." It is only after we conquer the money mind meld—the trancelike state that worshiping wealth induces—that we are able to identify our unique purpose, identity, and connections.

Armed with such knowledge, we can become experts at wielding the art of subtraction to balance the competing demands of delayed gratification and YOLO. Although life presents us with opportunities to rewrite our story and embrace second chances, it would be a tragedy to live life without paying homage to the urgency of now and even being frivolous at times.

In the second section we explored the parable of the three brothers. The parable is meant to be a resource as opposed to a step-by-step guide. Once armed with a strong sense of what *enough* is for us, we still need to understand how to create the economic power to fuel our journey. Indeed, there are many roads, many paths to financial independence. Whichever brother you may feel most connected to, the templates provide a way forward: front-loading, passive income, or the passion play. We must all build our own perpetual money machine so we can use our time and energy pursuing what is more important.

You get to decide which brother you want to be. You also get to change your mind as time passes. This process will help you not only get your own financial house in order, but also have those tough money conversations with your loved ones.

And in the last section of the book, we contemplated the ephemeral nature of time. We cannot commoditize time, but we can commoditize the activities we choose to fill it with. We can also use time perception hacks to get the most out of this short life. Because time waits for no one, we must become experts at investing ourselves far beyond what we do with our money—not only so that we don't have regrets as we lie on our deathbeds, but also so that we can enjoy the fruits of our labors: our jobs, education, friends, children, and physical and mental health.

While it may seem from the stories in this book that the dying are full of remorse and regrets, I have also had the privilege of being present for many peaceful and uplifting deaths. They help show us the power of addressing these issues and being intentional before one is diagnosed with a terminal illness.

Ronald waltzed in and out of my office over the years as if he had not a care in the world. He was the patriarch of a large family with a couple of kids and a handful of grandchildren. He was a successful business owner who had generated enough wealth through his chain of hardware stores to support generations into the future. He was a well-respected denizen of his community and was willing to lend not only his money but his time to whatever cause was most in need.

So it was with great surprise that I welcomed him into my office for what would end up to be our last time. He had lost significant weight; his face was gaunt and drawn. He had a look I had come to know over years of practicing medicine and counseling the elderly and frail. I knew immediately that death was near.

CAT scans and blood work showed metastatic pancreatic cancer spread throughout his abdominal cavity. As several generations of family members wept and lamented, Ronald faced his death sentence with his characteristic humility and dignity.

There would be no hospital beds, no chemotherapy, no IVs or procedures. There would be no hardship. He would die quietly at home—surrounded by the love of his family and friends.

He passed away several weeks later. I made a house call a few days before. Family and caretakers skittered frenetically about his bedroom as he leaned back into his recliner.

He was at ease.

In a moment of weakness, I uncharacteristically drew attention to his sense of calm and serenity. I asked haltingly: "I have watched many people die. How is it that you face death so comfortably?"

He looked up quietly with a hint of mirth dancing lazily at the corner of his lips. "Dying? Dying is the easy part."

And indeed, it was. Because he had faced pain, love, regret, and humility. He stared down the strange and daunting challenges that we all struggle with during *the climb* and built a life full of purpose, identity, and connections. Ronald had recognized and embraced "enough."

May you find similar peace in life as Ronald did in death.

I hope this book reaches you at a time when you are questioning the role that money and wealth play in your life. Over the years, I have learned countless lessons from taking care of the terminally ill. While there are too many to contain in one book, I have put together those that have touched me most and added indescribable value to my life.

The choice is yours. Whether you have reached a place of financial stability or are struggling to put tonight's dinner on the table, my hope is that the juxtaposition of what I have learned about life from taking care of the dying and what I have learned about money from studying financial independence can help you today—not tomorrow, not some time in the future, and certainly not while you are lying on your deathbed.

The writing of this book comes from a place of privilege. I enjoy not just the boon of having enough wealth to control which activities fill my time, but also the utter privilege of being invited into people's lives as they lay dying. My fervent hope is to pass on the knowledge I have gleaned to you.

My hope is to give you these secrets today and not twenty years from now—to effect change immediately, while you are still young and healthy. Before it's too late.

I have said more than once that we are constantly moving toward our eventual demise. *We are dying from the day we are born*—a truth that can't be denied or changed. But let me leave you with one last thought that is equally true:

We are living until the day we die.

Live well!

GLOSSARY

Bucket list: A number of experiences or achievements that a person hopes to have or accomplish during their lifetime.

Commodity: A raw material or primary agricultural product that can be bought and sold, such as copper or coffee. *Commoditize*: verb, to turn into a commodity.

Conservatorship: The appointment of a guardian by a judge to manage the financial affairs and daily life of another person due to old age or physical or mental limitations.

Deus ex machina: A plot device whereby a seemingly unsolvable problem in a story is suddenly and abruptly resolved by an unexpected and unlikely occurrence.

Efficient-market hypothesis: In financial economics, the hypothesis that asset prices reflect all available information.

Embrace the suck: Military term; to consciously accept or appreciate something that is extremely unpleasant but unavoidable for forward progress.

Emotional well-being: How you feel on a daily basis—what we commonly refer to as "happiness."

FI: Financial independence.

Fiduciary financial advisers: Advisers who manage client assets with the clients' best financial interests in mind.

Financial independence (FI): The status of having enough income to pay one's living expenses for the rest of one's life without having to be employed or dependent on others.

FIRE: Financial independence, retire early.

Form W-2: An Internal Revenue Service tax form used in the US to report wages paid to employees and the taxes withheld from them.

Four percent rule: Rule, created using historical data on stock and bond returns over a fifty-year period, that states you can withdraw 4 percent of your portfolio each year in retirement for a comfortable life.

Front-load: To distribute or allocate (costs, effort, and so on) unevenly, with the greater proportion at the beginning of the enterprise or process.

Geographic arbitrage: The process of moving from an area with a high cost of living area to an area with a low cost of living, so that spending less makes your money go further and supercharges your progress on the path to financial independence.

Golden handcuffs: Benefits, typically deferred payments, provided by an employer to discourage an employee from taking employment elsewhere or retiring.

Life evaluation: Long-term sense of accomplishment or satisfaction.

Limiting belief: Something you believe to be true about yourself, about others, or about the world that limits you in some way.

Modern portfolio theory: Also known as mean-variance analysis; a mathematical framework for assembling a portfolio of assets so that the expected return is maximized for a given level of risk.

Net worth: The total wealth of an individual, company, or household, taking account of all financial assets and liabilities.

Pareto Principle: The idea that eighty percent of our outcomes usually come from 20 percent of our work.

Parkinson's Law: The concept that the amount of time that one has to perform a task is the amount of time it will take to complete the task.

Probate: The judicial process whereby a will is "proved" in a court of law and accepted as a valid public document

Safe withdrawal rate (SWR): A method that calculates how much a retiree can draw annually from their accumulated assets without running out of money prior to death.

Side hustle: A means of making money alongside one's main form of employment or income.

Slow FI: When someone utilizes the incremental financial freedom they gain along the journey to financial independence to live a happier and healthier life, do better work, and build strong relationships.

SPIA: Single premium immediate annuity; a contract with an insurance company in which you give the insurance company a lump sum of money, and the insurance company pays you a set amount every month for the rest of your life.

Term life insurance or term assurance: Life insurance that provides coverage at a fixed rate of payments for a limited period of time, the relevant term.

White swan event: A common but unexpected event that has significant financial impacts on a person (for example, divorce, a death in the family, or illness).

Will or testament: A legal document that expresses a person's wishes about how their property is to be distributed after their death.

Work: Activities we do to create goods and services. *Employment* is the act of creating goods and services for another person or business, often in exchange for money.

YOLO: You only live once; "carpe diem," the idea that you should live life to the fullest regardless of cost.

ACKNOWLEDGMENTS

I was warned by almost all of my acquaintances who traveled this journey before me that writing a book would be an immensely challenging project. After all the blood, sweat, and tears, there are many who deserve a hearty thank-you for all the time, effort, and guidance they have supplied.

To Grant Sabatier, who chose to champion this project from the beginning. Your many hours spent discussing, reading, and rereading my manuscript have elevated the level of discourse to where it stands today. I would never have embarked on this journey nor come to its completion without all your help. Huge gratitude and love!

To Joe Saul-Sehy, for being a great creative partner and friend. You push me past the borders of comfort on a regular basis, and the product always comes out better than it started. Your tireless energy and creativity inspire me.

To J. L. Collins, for being an amazing friend and batting back and forth ideas with me on Zoom. Our conversations mean the world to me as does your incredible contribution to the personal finance world.

To Vicki Robin, who continues to inspire me daily. Your foreword made me so proud to have written this book. Thank you for caring about not only the personal finance world, but also humanity.

To my literary agent, Anna Geller. Thank you for pushing me, supporting me, advocating for me, and being the voice of reason when I was not able to be. You always make me feel fully supported and taken care of. This is more than I ever expected from an agent.

To the ever-talented Sarah Rainone, who wrangled my book ideas into a cohesive book proposal and narrative. You took my scrawlings as a long-time blog writer and helped me understand how to fashion them into the book that *Taking Stock* has become. I could never even have started without you.

To Claire Sielaff and the whole team over at Ulysses Press, who took this first-time author and showed him how to work with a publisher. I always found the team to be easy and inviting. You solicited my opinion and yet gave the difficult feedback when necessary.

To all the personal finance bloggers, podcasters, and content creators who have inspired and taught me. I am proud to call many of you my friends: Jillian Johnsrud, Dave from Accidental FIRE, Chad Metthner, Chris Mamula, Brad Barret, Jonathan Mendonsa, Paula Pant, Alma Lugtu, William McVey, Kerry Chevalier, Bill Yount, Airman Mildollar, Gwen Merz, Alan Donegan, Simon Paine, Kristy Shen, Bryce Leung, Pete Adeney, Cody Berman, Doug Nordman, Karsten Jeske, Jim Wang, Andy Hill, Chad "Coach" Carson, M. K. Williams, Jennifer Mah, Diania Merriam, Travis Shakespeare, J. D. Roth, Stephen Baughier, David Baughier, Leif Dahleen the Physician on FIRE, Tanja Hester, Paul Thompson, Jen Smith, Joel Laarsgard and Matt Altmix from How To Money, Carl and Mindy Jensen, and Kiersten and Julien Saunders for all your support.

To my lifelong friends Troy Foster, Jaspal Singh, and Stephen Young. Thank you for putting up with me all these years.

To my mom, dad, and stepdad for your relentless support, knowledge, and upbringing. Most of my good habits were learned long before I knew anything and came from watching you.

To Katie, Cameron, and Leila. You are my heart and soul, my day and night, my reason for waking up every morning. Thank you for being patient while this book distracted me from giving you my attentions. Sometimes I have a one-track mind.

ABOUT THE AUTHOR

Jordan Grumet was born in Evanston, Illinois, in 1973. His interest in becoming a doctor was ignited when his father, an oncologist, died unexpectedly in the prime of life. This profound loss not only inspired Jordan to practice medicine, but also has given him a unique perspective as a financial expert, challenging him to think deeply and critically about concepts like wealth, abundance, and financial independence.

After graduating from the University of Michigan, Jordan received his medical degree from Northwestern University and began practicing internal medicine in Northbrook, Illinois. He currently is an associate medical director at JourneyCare Hospice.

After years of blogging about financial independence and wellness, Jordan launched the *Earn & Invest* podcast in 2018. In 2019 he received the Plutus Award for Best New Personal Finance Podcast and was nominated in 2020 and 2021 for Best Personal Finance Podcast of the year.